# Language through Literature

**Creative**

**language**

**teaching**

**through**

**literature**

## Susan Bassnett and Peter Grundy

Pilgrims

Longman

**Longman Group UK Limited,**
*Longman House, Burnt Mill, Harlow,*
*Essex CM20 2JE, England*
*and Associated Companies throughout the world.*

© Longman Group UK Limited 1993

This book is produced in association
with Pilgrims Language Courses Limited
of Canterbury, England.

*All rights reserved, no part of this publication*
*may be reproduced, stored in a retrieval system,*
*or transmitted in any form or by any means, electronic,*
*mechanical, photocopying, recording or otherwise,*
*without the prior written permission of the Publishers.*

First published 1993

Set in 10/12pt ITC Cheltenham Book

Produced by Longman Singapore Publishers Pte Ltd

Printed in Singapore

**British Library Cataloguing in Publication Data**

McGuire Bassnett, Susan
   Language Through Literature: Creative
   Language Teaching Through Literature
   I. Title II. Grundy, Peter
   407.1

ISBN 0-582-07003-1

**Acknowledgements**
We are grateful to the following for permission to
reproduce copyright material:

Carcanet Press Ltd for the poems 'The Computer's First Christmas Card'
& 'The First Men on Mercury' by Edwin Morgan from *Collected Poems*;
Faber & Faber Ltd for the poem 'Hawk Roosting' from *Lupercal* by Ted Hughes
(1960) & 'Wild Oats' from *The Whitsun Weddings* by Philip Larkin (1964); Oxford
University Press for the poem 'A Martian Sends a Postcard Home' from
*A Martian Sends a Postcard Home* by Craig Raine (1979), © Craig Raine 1979;
the author, Anne Pechou for an adapted extract from *The Poet and the Scientists*
(Pilgrims Publications, 1985); Writers Forum for poems from *ABC in Sound* by
Bob Cobbing, © Writers Forum 1965, included in *Alphabet and Letter Poems*
edited by Peter Mayer (The Menard Press, 1978)

We have been unable to trace the copyright holders in the following & would
appreciate any information that would enable us to do so;
the poem 'Address' by Alurista; the poem 'Responsibility' by Peter Appleton;
the poem 'Reported Missing' by Barry Cole; *The Literary Practice Handbook*
by Barry Palmer(1984); an article about loud music on coaches and buses.

**Illustrations** by Kathy Baxendale

**Cover illustrated** by Helen Manning

## A letter from the Series Editors

Dear Teacher,

This series of teachers' resource books has developed from Pilgrims' involvement in running courses for learners of English and for teachers and teacher trainers.

Our aim is to pass on ideas, techniques and practical activities which we know work in the classroom. Our authors, both Pilgrims' teachers and like-minded colleagues in other organisations, present accounts of innovative procedures which will broaden the range of options available to teachers working within communicative and humanistic approaches.

We would be very interested to receive your impressions of the series. If you notice any omissions that we ought to record in future editions, or if you think of any interesting variations, please let us know. We will be glad to acknowledge all contributions that we are able to use.

*Seth Lindstromberg*
Series Editor

*Mario Rinvolucri*
Series Consultant

Pilgrims Language Courses
Canterbury
Kent
CT1 3HG
England

## Susan Bassnett

## Peter Grundy

Susan was educated in several countries, including Denmark, Portugal and Italy, and spent much of her youth picking up the various languages she encountered along the way. She is currently Professor of Comparative Literary Theory at the University of Warwick, where she runs the post-graduate degrees in Translation Studies, Comparative Literary Theory, and British Cultural Studies. She specialises in intercultural work, and has lectured and held workshops in universities and colleges throughout the world. Susan has written several academic works including *Translation Studies* (1980 Routledge), *Translation, History and Culture*, with André Lefevère (1990 Pinter), and *Elizabeth I: A Feminist Biography* (1988 Berg). She also has considerable experience of teaching creative writing to adults, is herself a poet and translator, and has four children.

Peter studied Literature at the University of Leeds, Education at the University of Oxford, and Linguistics at the University of Cambridge. He has taught in schools in Britain and Germany and worked in initial teacher training for a number of years at the College of St Hild and St Bede, Durham. He currently teaches Applied Linguistics and Pragmatics at the University of Durham, where he specialises in second language acquisition theory and language teaching methodology. He is also particularly interested in introducing learner-centred approaches to the teaching of English for Academic Purposes. In addition to this, he is a director and teacher on summer schools in Britain and has written several books with Arthur Brookes, including *Designer Writing* (1988 Pilgrims Publications) and *Writing for Study Purposes* (1990 CUP).

# Contents

Index of activities     vi

Acknowledgements     viii

**Introduction**     1

---

**Chapter 1** Differences and discoveries     11

**Chapter 2** One text     32

**Chapter 3** Pre-reading     50

**Chapter 4** Reading     67

**Chapter 5** Translation     80

**Chapter 6** Writing     91

**Chapter 7** Beginners     110

**Chapter 8** Advanced learners     120

Bibliography     136

# Index of activities

| | ACTIVITY | LEVEL (+ = the level stated or above) |
|---|---|---|
| **1 DIFFERENCES AND DISCOVERIES** | 1.1 Meeting poem | Elementary + |
| | 1.2 Concentration | Elementary + |
| | 1.3 Exotic objects | Elementary + |
| | 1.4 Openers | Higher elementary + |
| | 1.5 Telling stories | Higher elementary + |
| | 1.6 Red Indian names | Higher elementary + |
| | 1.7 My turn, your turn | Higher elementary + |
| | 1.8 Name pairs | Intermediate + |
| | 1.9 Picture prompting | Beginner + |
| | 1.10 Reworking stories | Intermediate + |
| | 1.11 Retelling stories | Intermediate + |
| | 1.12 Mirroring stories | Intermediate + |
| | 1.13 Gender pronouns | Intermediate + |
| | 1.14 Breaking the mood | Beginner + |
| | 1.15 Jigsaw lines | Intermediate + |
| | 1.16 Reshaping poems | Intermediate + |
| | 1.17 The first men on Mercury | Intermediate + |
| **2 ONE TEXT** | 2.1 Predicting | Elementary + |
| | 2.2 Grouping | Elementary + |
| | 2.3 Exchanging | Higher elementary + |
| | 2.4 Assessing | Higher elementary/Intermediate + |
| | 2.5 Translating | Elementary + |
| | 2.6 Exemplifying | Intermediate + |
| | 2.7 Visualising | Elementary + |
| | 2.8 Associating | Higher elementary + |
| | 2.9 Meaning | Higher elementary + |
| | 2.10 Contributing | Higher elementary–Advanced |
| | 2.11 Clozing | Higher elementary + |
| | 2.12 Substituting | Intermediate + |
| | 2.13 Contrasting | Higher elementary + |
| | 2.14 Completing | Higher elementary/Intermediate |
| | 2.15 Evaluating | Beginner/Elementary + |
| | 2.16 Reducing | Beginner + |
| **3 PRE-READING** | 3.1 Poem and collage | Beginner + |
| | 3.2 Taking sides | Intermediate + |
| | 3.3 Supplying the answers | Intermediate + |
| | 3.4 Profiling the writer | Intermediate + |
| | 3.5 Poems and their word sets | Intermediate + |
| | 3.6 The unexpected | Elementary + |
| | 3.7 Restoring the original | Intermediate + |
| | 3.8 Understanding unusual texts | Higher intermediate + |
| **4 READING** | 4.1 Adverbs and fiction | Elementary–Intermediate |
| | 4.2 Asking naive questions | Intermediate + |
| | 4.3 Gossiping | Intermediate + |
| | 4.4 Relating | Elementary + |
| | 4.5 Poetical chairs | Elementary + |
| | 4.6 Improving texts | Intermediate + |
| | 4.7 Reflecting | Intermediate + |
| | 4.8 Before and after | Intermediate + |
| | 4.9 Layers of meaning | Intermediate + |
| | 4.10 Key words | Beginner + |
| | 4.11 Jigsaw reading | Intermediate + |

| | | ACTIVITY | LEVEL |
|---|---|---|---|
| **5** | **TRANSLATION** | 5.1 Language and pictures | Intermediate |
| | | 5.2 Idiotic idioms | Intermediate + |
| | | 5.3 International jokes | Intermediate + |
| | | 5.4 Wise sayings | Elementary + |
| | | 5.5 Words and their weight | Intermediate + |
| | | 5.6 What gets lost | Elementary + |
| | | 5.7 Poetry reversi | Intermediate + |
| | | 5.8 Translationese | Higher intermediate + |
| | | 5.9 Chinese poem | Intermediate + |
| | | 5.10 Bilingual poems | Higher intermediate + |
| **6** | **WRITING** | 6.1 Shape poems | Higher elementary + |
| | | 6.2 My poem is me | Higher elementary + |
| | | 6.3 Frames | Higher elementary + |
| | | 6.4 Autobiography in objects | Higher elementary + |
| | | 6.5 Sounds of words | Intermediate + |
| | | 6.6 Writing about work | Advanced |
| | | 6.7 Comic or tragic? | Intermediate + |
| | | 6.8 Object and character | Intermediate + |
| | | 6.9 Three wishes | Intermediate + |
| | | 6.10 Genres | Intermediate + |
| | | 6.11 Fifty-word novel | Intermediate + |
| | | 6.12 Syllable poems | Intermediate + |
| | | 6.13 Cloning with a difference | Intermediate + |
| | | 6.14 Writing from starters | Beginner + |
| | | 6.15 Newspaper poetry | Intermediate + |
| | | 6.16 Composite poems | Higher intermediate + |
| | | 6.17 Drama as speech act | Intermediate + |
| **7** | **BEGINNERS** | 7.1 Sounds | Beginner/Elementary |
| | | 7.2 Words | Beginner/Elementary |
| | | 7.3 Rhymes | Beginner/Elementary |
| | | 7.4 Lines | Beginner/Elementary |
| | | 7.5 Likeness | Beginner/Elementary |
| | | 7.6 Sounds that are similar | Beginner/Elementary |
| | | 7.7 Words that fit | Beginner/Elementary |
| | | 7.8 Response | Beginner/Elementary |
| | | 7.9 Peripheral learning | Beginner/Elementary |
| **8** | **ADVANCED LEARNERS** | 8.1 Alphabet poems | Advanced |
| | | 8.2 The great lie | Higher intermediate + |
| | | 8.3 Alphabet sentences | Higher intermediate + |
| | | 8.4 Variations on a text | Higher intermediate + |
| | | 8.5 A crisis twice | Advanced |
| | | 8.6 Subjectivity-objectivity | Advanced |
| | | 8.7 Streams of consciousness | Advanced |
| | | 8.8 Brave new worlds | Advanced |
| | | 8.9 Signifying with sounds | Advanced |
| | | 8.10 Everyday rhythms | Higher intermediate + |
| | | 8.11 Proverbs of hell | Higher intermediate + |
| | | 8.12 Writing the unwritable | Advanced |
| | | 8.13 Discussing a text | Higher intermediate + |

# ACKNOWLEDGEMENTS

We would like to acknowledge a considerable debt to a great many people. Over the years, we have worked with colleagues engaged in teaching in various parts of the world. Ideas have been exchanged, borrowed and loaned, and modifications have occurred as exercises have been adapted for specific purposes. We have all been engaged for so long in this happy process that it becomes extremely difficult to trace the origins of many of the ideas in *Language through Literature*.

To anyone whose name is not mentioned here and who picks up this book and finds an exercise they believe was their original idea we apologise. We have used these exercises for so long that we have come to feel them as ours, though obviously we cannot repeat too often that work of this kind cannot be seen as anyone's property because we are all engaged in the business of sharing and spreading ideas.

We each belong to working communities and different professional networks which have enabled us to work creatively and develop ideas alongside colleagues whose imaginative and thoughtful approaches have been a constant inspiration. We owe particular debts to our colleagues and students at the two Universities – Durham and Warwick – where we work. Several generations of students – native speakers and non-native speakers – have provided invaluable opportunities for us to try out and refine materials as well as giving us feedback of exceptional quality: this book would not have been possible without such enthusiasm.

Among the individuals and working communities that we would like to single out for special thanks are John Broadbent, Barry Palmer and David Punter, founder members of the DUET (Development of University English Teaching project) at the University of East Anglia, whose conferences have made such a contribution to new approaches to literary studies; Anne Cluysenaar, founder member of the Verbal Arts Association, whose work in creative writing has been inspirational; Andrew Davies, who always brought such energy, good humour and clever ideas to the Warwick Writers' Workshops; and Clive Barker and Sue Jennings, whose work in actor training and dramatherapy respectively has inspired a number of our own exercises.

In the area of language teaching methodology, we owe a great deal to the many Pilgrims colleagues who have been so generous in sharing their innovative ideas. In so far as we are able, we have tried to continue the Pilgrims example of collaborative teaching, originality and learner-centred methodology.

Finally, we are grateful for the enabling encouragement and finely-tuned judgment of Seth Lindstromberg, our series editor, and Marion Cooper, Janet Aitchison and Lisa Howard, our publishers at Longman. We are also grateful to our editor, Brigit Viney, whose careful reading of the manuscript saved us from many embarrassments, and for Mario Rinvolucri's sharp comments on the first draft of our Introduction and John Morgan's five-page essay on what to do about them.

# Introduction

## APPROACH

We begin our description of the approach this book follows by listing what were the starting points for us. They were:

1 Our belief that literature should be part of a complete language learning experience.
2 Our concern about approaches to literature which place understanding texts ahead of seeing the learner as a resource and working from that learner's store of experience and intuitive poetic awareness.
3 Our refusal to agree that 'creative writing' is something done by others, and that language learner writing should be something more akin to analysis and paraphrase. We believe writing should be taught as basic literary practice.
4 Our feeling that there is a need for a methodology change in the teaching of 'foreign' literature, to bring it more into line with the learner-centred, collaborative approach of the communicative method.
5 Our disagreement with language teachers who say that they are uncertain about the classroom possibilities that literature can provide, and equally our frustration with literature teachers who ignore language.
6 Our feeling that there is a need for more original, worthwhile and effective ideas for using literature in language teaching, and especially ideas based on principled linguistic and methodological rationales.

Our ideas for this book developed directly out of language teaching experience, and out of a shared sense that we needed to find new ways of working with literature in language teaching. We both felt strongly that the division which has arisen between the teaching of literature and the teaching of language is not only an unhappy one, it is also a false one. We have encountered language teachers who think literature is irrelevant, who argue that what students need are texts that are 'practical' and 'rooted in everyday experience', not works of art. And we have encountered literature teachers who look down on 'mere language' work, as though literary texts were made of some ethereal matter and not constructed out of language at all.

We want to reject attitudes which we feel are prejudiced and we want to find ways of helping teachers who do want to bridge the gap between these two extreme positions. There are already lots of anthologies of literary works that teachers can use, and so this book is designed differently. We do not want to show people 'how to' read literature, as though there were a right way and a wrong way. Literary criticism over the past twenty years or so has very firmly eliminated the old idea that there is a 'correct' way to read in order to find out what the author intended. Now, the role of the reader is recognised as being of crucial importance. When the language learner approaches a literary text, he or she should do so not in a spirit of humility (the 'how- will-I-ever-understand-what-such-a-great-writer-has-written' approach) but in a spirit of discovery. As the reader explores literature, so not only do new worlds open up in the imagination, but new layers of language used and new examples of linguistic dexterity are exposed. When we read Shakespeare it should not be because he is regarded as a master, but because his skill in using language is a pleasure to be enjoyed.

## Who is this book for?

*Language through Literature* will be useful to you whether you teach literature or language. It will be useful if you teach literature because it contains dozens of new ideas which you can use to enable your students to read the set texts they have to study on more equal terms. Rather than treating the literature syllabus as a kind of advanced comprehension exercise, our approach looks beyond the language barrier that many literary texts pose and helps your students to understand literature by working creatively with texts.

*Language through Literature* will also be useful to you if you are a language teacher because it contains a wealth of straightforward, imaginative activities at all levels which will provide your students with real opportunities to produce writing whose quality will astonish and delight them.

In addition, the exercises in this book will help your students to appreciate the poetic dimension of the everyday language they want to acquire. For example, in Britain there is a well-known chain store called *Marks and Spencer*. It is no coincidence that when Michael Marks and Tom Spencer started their business, they decided to call it *Marks and Spencer* rather than *Spencer and Marks*. This stylistic preference reflects in a very simple way the poetry of everyday language. And if this isn't proof enough, if you live in Britain, you will know that *Marks and Spencer* has a nickname, *Marks and Sparks*. This small example, one amongst many we could have chosen, shows the fundamentally poetic nature of all everyday language use. Developing intuitions as to stylistic preferences of this sort is an important part of second language learning. The activities in *Language through Literature* are a short-cut to developing this sort of intuition about everyday English.

Because we conceive of the reader as an active participant, this book quite deliberately includes exercises in writing as well as reading. We have included a number of exercises that may well be called 'creative writing' exercises, and again we have done this because we reject the assumption that 'creative' work belongs outside the language learning classroom. It is often assumed that the language learner is somehow unfit to write poetry for example, and should keep to analysing texts or paraphrasing them. We do not want to minimise the importance of analysis and paraphrase, but we also believe that the best way to read is to learn to write, and likewise the best way to write is to learn to read. The exercises in this book have been carefully selected in terms of difficulty, and teachers are provided with detailed explanations of how each activity works. By putting creative writing firmly back into the language learning classroom, along with close reading of literary texts, we feel sure that the enjoyment of teachers and students will be increased.

*Language through Literature* is for the kind of teacher who is looking for classroom activities which are experiential and which involve groups of learners in working collaboratively and making their own personal discoveries. Although you will find a number of well-tried ideas in this book, most of the activities will be new to you.

## How this book works

We have divided the book into eight chapters, each containing as few as eight or as many as seventeen different activities. We have called these activities 'exercises', but they are not exercises in the sense of being habitual or mechanical or because they make students jump through hoops. They are 'exercises' because they are part of a continuous, skill-building practice. Just as in dance the performer practises exercises on the way to perfection, so in language learning technical and exploratory exercises are part of the practice that makes perfect.

In general, this book makes many practical suggestions for the integration of *literary practice* into the general language classroom. We do not suggest an explicit methodology for a *literature syllabus*; indeed, by implication we argue for a syllabus that is centred more on method or approach than on subject matter. This view of the changing nature of syllabus design – that method/approach cannot any longer be sensibly distinguished from content/material – has been steadily gaining ground in recent years and is developed in detail in David Nunan's work in particular (Nunan 1988a and b). On the whole we accept this position and see the method/approach as more important than, and not absolutely divisible from, the material we work with. Even if you are a teacher working with a traditional literature syllabus that specifies a list of set texts, we are confident that our methods and approaches will work well in your given work context. And if you are a language teacher who never expected to use literature in the classroom, we hope this book will persuade you to give it a try.

## How to get the best out of this book

We have provided detailed step-by-step instructions for implementing each exercise in the classroom. We have also included a short section in each exercise which describes the aim of the exercise and often reflects an important linguistic, critical or pedagogic principle as well. This section and the Note that is sometimes included at the end of an exercise are designed to stimulate thought about the particular exercise and provide ideas for language teaching in general.

Within each chapter, the exercises are sequenced from those which work from the learners' knowledge or experience to those which are based on text. This does not mean you have to work through a chapter from the beginning to the end – just go ahead and pick exercises that appeal to you and that practise a skill that is important to your students.

A key concept in this book is the creative power of surprise. We have tried to design exercises that will surprise students, that will break preconceived patterns of expectation and experience and invite them to try their hand at a very varied range of linguistic activity. Many of the exercises can be used in the first language classroom too, in teaching writing for example, because they enable students to develop their creative potential as well as extending their linguistic competence.

We hope that as you use this book, you and your students will derive not only instruction but also entertainment from it. We believe that a crucial component of learning is the pleasure that learning can generate, and if just one student somewhere in the world goes home rejoicing in the fact that he or she has managed to write a tiny poem in English, then this book will have served its purpose.

# METHODOLOGY

The first part of this Introduction could be compared to the telephone book, in the sense that one goes to it for information one expects to find in it in advance. Precisely the opposite is the case with a novel or poem. We hope that the second and third parts of the Introduction, which are about methodology and about literature and language, will be more unpredictable.

As we wrote this book, we had a number of teaching objectives and classroom options in mind. We think these are important for language teaching in general and because they play such an important part in our thinking, we have arranged them as a kind of 'manifesto' addressed to ourselves. Why don't you read each 'clause' and see what you think: Yes; No; Not sure?

　1 **Autonomy:** The purpose of teaching is to help learners to reach the stage where they can operate autonomously, i.e. without teachers.

2 **Control and initiative:** Learner initiative is more important than teacher control.

3 **Learner-centredness:** This means thinking first of the learners, their abilities, interests, learning styles, personalities, immediate language needs, and second of the material or methods, which will be consequent on the first.

4 **Goals:** No one knows what language or how much of it should or can be taught because no one knows how to quantify the outcome of successful second language learning. This holds true for working with literature too.

5 **Individualisation:** The learning experience and the actual language acquired will always be slightly different for every learner. We should encourage each student to learn what is good for them.

6 **The roles of teachers and learners:** These will be constantly changing. The perceived gap between teacher and learner should be as small as possible because the more authoritarian the teacher, the less self-respect the learner retains. The less self-respect the learner retains, the less the learner is motivated. Roles that teachers do not need to assume include determiner of what is to be learnt, knower, authority figure, performer, and provider of the language the learners were supposed to be providing.

7 **Motivation:** Learners-by-choice are more motivated than learners-by-compulsion.

8 **Resources:** The prime classroom resources are the learner's knowledge and experience of life, and the learner's in-built syllabus which determines the order in which structures will be acquired.

9 **Modelling language:** Teaching model structures has its roots in behaviouristic psychology which is now known to be much inferior to self-discovery in promoting effective learning. We want our learners to find ways of expressing the meanings that are important to them: we do not want them to repeat rehearsed responses.

10 **Affect:** We need to recognise and respect the learner's emotional responses to the language, to literature, to the learning situation and to the target culture.

11 **Innateness and readiness:**
   - We are all equally capable of acquiring a second language but we are not all equally ready to start doing so.
   - We all have strong personal feelings but we are not all equally ready to share them.
   - We are all equally able to respond and contribute but we are not all equally ready to do so.

12 **Collaboration:** If a team of teachers works together, each member shares the responsibility for the work that goes on in the classroom. In the same way, learners working collaboratively tend to be less anxious and more productive.

13 **Silence:** An increasing number of teachers and applied linguists agree that a 'silent period' in the early stages of second language learning enables learners to work out a rule system for the target

language. This silent period may be as important as the silent period before the onset of speech in first language acquisition. From a humanistic perspective too, the learner's right to silence should be respected. This is more than ever true when it comes to sharing writing, where inevitably some learners will sometimes be unwilling to share their half-made work with others. A good way of respecting the learner writer's right to silence at times when writing is shared is for each member of the class to have an opportunity to read their work or to say 'Pass' and thereafter remain silent. Lastly, there are also silences which it is not appropriate for anyone, teacher or learner, to fill.

## RATIONALE

In this final section we raise four issues of importance for language teachers who are thinking about the role of literature in their class-rooms.

### How does literature relate to everyday language?

It is common knowledge that the English talk a lot about the weather. Students learn phrases such as 'Nice day, isn't it?' or 'I think it might rain later' or 'It's a lovely day today'. They are told that these phrases will be useful in all kinds of social situations, in shops, on trains, at parties, and many people are pleasantly surprised when they come to England and find that this is indeed the case. But when they do come to England, they discover something else as well, i.e. the reason for so many polite formulae about the weather. Since English weather is so unpredictable, and since the cloudscapes overhead are always so magnificently varied, the question of what the weather will do has real meaning. In a country where the weather can be predicted with some accuracy there is no need to talk about it, but in Britain generally, nobody can fail to take an interest in the erratic weather conditions.

Students with some degree of expertise in English soon discover that this national obsession with the weather has left lasting traces in English vocabulary, quite apart from the polite formulaic phrases. For example, English abounds with verbs describing nuances of light and light on water – *shine, shimmer, sparkle, glitter, glimmer, gleam, glisten* – and so on. All these words differ subtly in meaning and in most other European languages they can all be translated into two or three verbs and no more. The weather, the constant rain and the greyness that characterise an English winter (and sometimes an English summer too) have led to developments in the language that enable a speaker to distinguish delicate shifts in the description of light. A poet writing in English has all these words from which to choose; the poet's 'word-hoard', to use a term that derives from Anglo-Saxon poetic convention, is full of near-but-not-quite-synonyms that allow for variety of expression.

There are a lot of poems in English about the weather – a great many cloud poems, poems about rain and wind, poems about the way in which emotional states are prefigured by climatic states. 'Frost froze the land, hail fell on earth then, corn of the coldest' wrote Ezra Pound in his translation of the Anglo-Saxon poem 'The Seafarer' in which an outcast bemoans his hard lot in life, and the anonymous medieval author of 'Come blow, come blow thou wild west wind' uses typical English winter weather as an image for his love sickness. In prose too, the weather features strongly. The storm wind is one of the protagonists in *Wuthering Heights*, like the fog in Charles Dickens's *Bleak House* or the rain in some of Thomas Hardy's novels.

We began with a simple sentence about the day's weather, 'Nice day, isn't it?', a standard phrase-book sentence in English, and have moved into the work of some of the greatest English novelists with practically no effort at all. In the same way, anyone learning English (or any other language) moves into literature because literature is a high point of language usage; arguably it marks the greatest skills a language user can demonstrate. Anyone who wants to acquire a profound knowledge of a language that goes beyond the utilitarian will read literary texts in that language.

Once we have begun to acquire some knowledge of a language, we need to know something about what we can do with that language. One of the best ways to explore these possibilities is by looking at the work of writers who, at different moments in the history of a culture, have explored that language to their best ability and so have extended the boundaries of its use. When we teach literature, what we are actually teaching is highly skilful language usage, and as we read literary texts we can study the ways in which a craftsman can shape language and make it richer and more powerful. When we teach English, we are not only teaching a language, but we are also teaching students about what that language can do. It may seem a long way from learning how to ask for a cup of tea to learning how to write a poem, but once the process is under way, the gap between those two activities narrows. It is significant that in English, for example, as in many other languages, even those people who claim they never read poetry and certainly never write it, actually turn to poetry on special occasions. Birthday cards, anniversary cards, Valentine cards and sympathy cards all frequently contain messages written in verse. The language of religious rites is a poetic language, and the language of all those important lay occasions – the wedding reception, the award-giving ceremony, the public speech, to name but a few, is essentially a literary language. We are all involved in making and reading literature, whether we realise it or not.

This may be because even our first attempts to speak have a literary quality. The onset of speech usually occurs when we are between nine months and three years old. Although speech first appears at different ages in different children, its course is much the same for all of us. Typically we begin with strings of vowel sounds (*a-a-a-a*) before moving on to strings of consonant-vowel combinations (*ma-ma-ma-ma, ba-ba-ba-ba, da-da-da-da*). Some of these are identifiable as our first words, the words for *mother* and *father*.

As more and more words are added, we typically produce language which differs in many obvious ways from the adult form. This is particularly true in phonology, where consonant clusters are simplified (/puːn/ for *spoon*), harmonies abound (/ʃiʃ/ for *fish*), the order of phonemes is swapped around (/efelənt/ for *elephant*), and polysyllabic words are reduced by eliminating the first unstressed syllable (/brelə/ for *umbrella* and /aːmdiləʊ/ for *armadillo*). Frequently more than one of these simplifying rules will be applied to a single word, so that one two-year-old friend of ours produced /klɒptə/ for *helicopter*, both reducing the number of syllables and swapping phonemes around.

One result of these simplifications is that child phonology is more harmonious than adult phonology. In accordance with this principle, one of the earliest phrases produced by one of our children was /di gəʊ bæ/. Each word begins with a stop sound and all the words share the same consonant–vowel structure. The adult version, *This old man* (as in the nursery rhyme, 'This old man / He played one / He played knick-knack/On my drum'), is a much less harmonious, or less poetic structure. Put another way, child language, or 'babytalk' as most people call it, is a form of poetry.

We began with our first words, *ma-ma* and *da-da*, and in no time at all were making a connection with the essential nature of poetry. Literature has its roots in everyday experience much more than is sometimes realised.

A fundamental principle of this book is that literature, both literary practice and working with texts, should be part of everyday second language acquisition work. And yet most of us who teach English as a second language have tended to put literature into a separate compartment for advanced, specialist learners. We have elevated speaking over writing, and especially over creative writing. We think of literature as representing the values of the culture. In all these ways, we have failed to remember just how everyday literature actually is.

## Isn't literature for advanced learners only?

No. You will find nearly as many exercises for beginner/elementary students as for intermediate and advanced ones in this book. In some ways this is the most radical difference between this book and all the other literature books that are at all comparable. No other book that we know of states that literature is for early-stage as well as advanced learners. This is very odd, bearing in mind the striking similarities we have seen between child language acquisition and literature. Many applied linguists believe that in acquiring a second language we first take a step back from our mother tongue. This enables us to reactivate a language learning 'device' which in turn enables us to acquire a syntax and a phonology different from those of our mother tongue. This is the childlike state where the harmonies, the poetic structures, the 'music' of a language, as Gattegno (1972, 1976) called it, are more obvious to us than at any other stage in second language learning. At this time, more than at any other, we are receptive to literature. The more advanced we become, the less accessible, the less useful, literature will be.

## 'Speaking comes before writing'

Although at first sight this seems unarguable, we will try to show that it's actually a much more doubtful idea than one might think. In theoretical linguistics, Chomskyan linguists try to describe the 'competence' or knowledge about language that each 'idealised native *speaker*' has. Almost all language teaching methodologies place listening and speaking ahead of reading and writing. Many people, if asked to give an opinion about writing, will tell you that writing is a debased form of speech and a partial representation of what talk sounds like.

Why is it doubtful to claim that speaking comes before writing? Basically, because to make this claim is to misunderstand the nature of 'writing'. It may seem odd at first to say that 'writing' turns up in both literate and non-literate societies. Yet the poet of the *Iliad* and the *Odyssey* was not literate and his (or her) poems had to wait several centuries before they were written down. All societies have a wide variety of non-literal or poetic language uses, and in non-literate societies these are not, for obvious reasons, ever written down.

In literate societies then, we tend to think of writing as representing speech, which of course it sometimes does, just as speech can represent writing. But actually it might be more sensible to use the word 'writing', whether in literate or non-literate societies, to describe the most striking examples of our innate ability to combine linguistic tokens creatively, whether in 'speech' or in 'writing'.

This perspective on 'writing', that it is a *natural*, *creative*, *original* and perhaps *primary* use of language, surely argues for the importance of literature (or 'writing') in the language classroom.

## 'Literature enshrines the values of a society'

Where does this idea come from? And what consequences follow from accepting it?

It is tempting to say that the rise of the nation state has led us to think in terms of national literatures and 'great' writers. So someone else's literature will convey, not universal values, but the values of their own cultures. This point is made very forcefully by Ngugi wa Thiongo'o in his paper 'Literature in Schools' (1986):

The teaching of only European literature, and mostly British imperialist literature, in our schools means that our students are daily being confronted with the European reflection of itself, the European image, in history. Our children are made to look at, analyse and evaluate the world as made and seen by Europeans. Worse still, these children are confronted with a distorted image of themselves and of their history as reflected and interpreted in European imperialist literature. They see how Prospero sees Caliban and not how Caliban sees Prospero; how Crusoe discovers and remakes Man Friday in Crusoe's image, but never how Friday views himself and his heroic struggles against centuries of Crusoe's exploitation and oppression.

In this quotation, Ngugi wa Thiongo'o complains about the way most literature teaching excludes those who do not belong and represents only a partial view of the world.

It often suits us well to see ourselves as members of a nation, or of a community – political, religious or perhaps just constituted by the town, village or even street where we live. The problem is that such communities exclude those with different backgrounds and perspectives.

Recently Mary Louise Pratt has challenged this notion of 'community' (Pratt 1987). She calls it an idealisation related to notions like 'fraternity' and 'nation state' and suggests instead that we need a 'linguistics of contact', which studies the interaction between those who do not share common ground. It is only because a speaker of British English and a speaker of American English come into contact, for example, that they realise which variety they speak, or indeed that they speak a variety at all. It is precisely this contact with the other which gives them their sense of group membership and linguistic identity.

All too often, therefore, we create literature out of innate, universal, human skills and then think of it as conveying the values of a particular community or culture.

This book is written very much against that spirit: we reject the quasi-imperialistic notion of accepted readings and the need to serve an apprenticeship before being accepted into the community of those who can read English literature with an English understanding. Instead, our exercises focus precisely on what happens when readers and writers with very different languages and cultures come into contact. We believe that everyone, even – no, especially – early-stage second language learners, can read literature and write creatively.

*Susan Bassnett*
*Peter Grundy*
*February 1993*

# CHAPTER 1

# *Differences and discoveries*

Every stage in the process of learning, from the baby struggling to make intelligible sounds to the postgraduate student completing a doctoral thesis, involves dealing with things that are different, and consequently in making new discoveries. The fearfulness that awareness of difference can at first provoke begins to disappear as we become more familiar with the new and move on, but the sense of excitement generated by discovery can stay with us so long as we continue to undergo different experiences without prejudice.

The exercises in this section are all concerned in one way or another with exploring difference. Many of them can be used when a group is first assembled, since they provide ways of establishing group identity and enabling students to feel at ease with the teacher and with one another. Another purpose of the exercises in this chapter is that of breaking down inhibitions in the classroom and encouraging students to use their new linguistic skills in more imaginative ways. The principle behind the exercises is a simple one: students of all ages work best when they are working creatively, when they are actively involved in the process and not passive receivers of information or instruction.

If you use this book quite early in a course, you will find that students gain confidence rapidly as they start to acquire a collection of creative texts that they have made themselves. Some of the exercises also involve training students to listen carefully: another skill that is essential to the language learner and one which can be inhibited both by shyness and by uneasiness when students come into contact with an unfamiliar culture.

As with all subsequent chapters, the exercises are organised in a specific order that does not so much reflect increased difficulty, but rather a deliberate attempt to move organically through different stages in the language learning process.

## 1.1

**TIME**
20 minutes
(depending on
class size)

**LEVEL**
Elementary +

**CLASS SIZE**
Any size up to 24.
Over this number
it becomes very
cumbersome and
loses its impact

# MEETING POEM

The object of this activity is two-fold. Firstly, it is a light-hearted way of introducing students to one another which also helps to build their confidence, since everybody ends up with a short poem. Secondly, it helps you discover something about the state of mind of the students; the results can indicate who is feeling particularly timid, who has a low self-image, etc.

## Procedure

1 Write your name on the board twice, using no more than two names. Set out the names as follows:

| SUSAN BASSNETT | PETER GRUNDY |
|---|---|
| 1 ........................................ | 1 ........................................ |
| 2 ........................................ | 2 ........................................ |
| 3 ........................................ | 3 ........................................ |
| SUSAN BASSNETT | PETER GRUNDY |

2 Ask each student to write two of their names in the same way on a piece of paper, leaving three blank lines between the two sets of names.

3 Ask the students to fill in the blank lines following these rules: they must write three lines; each line must consist of only two words; these two words must begin with the same letters as the letters of their name. So the above poems would look like this:

| SUSAN BASSNETT | PETER GRUNDY |
|---|---|
| SUPER BREADMAKER | PARTICULARLY GRUMPY |
| SIMPLY BEWILDERED | PATIENT GREEDY |
| STILL BREATHING | POOR GUY |
| SUSAN BASSNETT | PETER GRUNDY |

4 When the students have finished their poems, ask everyone to read their poem aloud to the group. This activity acts as a mnemonic and helps fix names in people's minds.

**VARIATION**
This can become a gift-giving exercise where students write two word phrases for each other's poems and then exchange them.

ACKNOWLEDGEMENT
We learnt this activity from the writer Andrew Davies.

# CONCENTRATION

In the Introduction (page 2), we discussed the poetic nature of everyday language, and pointed out that *Marks and Spencer*, for example, is more poetic than *Spencer and Marks*, although *Marks and Sparks* (as the shop is affectionately known in Britain) is best of all. This exercise, which should be used at the start of a lesson, is a way of drawing attention to the natural poetic function of everyday language. It also promotes group concentration and aesthetic awareness.

**1.2**

**TIME**
10 minutes

**LEVEL**
Elementary +

## Procedure

1 Ask the students to sit in a circle. Encourage them to work with their eyes shut. Explain that you are going to work in English and that you hope others will too but that mother-tongue contributions are also perfectly acceptable.
2 Explain that you will begin by saying the name of a multinational company aloud. Speak carefully and deliberately. Your neighbour will then continue with his or her choice of another multinational company and so on round the circle. For example:

Teacher:   Shell
Student 1: Texaco
Student 2: ICI

3 When everyone in the circle has named a multinational company and it is your turn again, change the category by saying, for example, 'Types of food: roast beef and Yorkshire pudding'. Your neighbour then continues in this new category.
4 Introduce four or five new categories. With each new category, the mood of concentration, the fluency and the consciousness of the poetic element should strengthen. Other suitable categories include high-street shops, birthplaces, a couple I know well, my mother's or father's forenames, football teams.

# EXOTIC OBJECTS

The aim of this exercise is to show how a poem can be made simply from a list of words suggested by an exotic object. Some people produce much better poems than others in this exercise. Even for those students whose poems are not so successful, the exercise reveals possibilities for writing as shown in their colleagues' poems.

**1.3**

**TIME**
35–40 minutes

**LEVEL**
Elementary +

**MATERIALS**
One exotic object for each group of 6 students

## Preparation

Set the classroom out so that each exotic object is on a table surrounded by six chairs.

## Procedure

1 Ask the students to sit at a table where there is an object they have never seen before.
2 Tell each student to tear three or four sheets of paper into forty or fifty small pieces. Ask each student to think of as many words as possible which they can associate with the object on their table. Every time they think of a word, they should write it on one of the small pieces of paper and place it on the table.
3 Tell the group to arrange the words alphabetically on the table.
4 Each student then chooses a number of the words (maybe around twenty) with which to make a poem. It is a good idea to suggest that the students first begin choosing words by trying to choose a word beginning with each letter from A to Z but that they can abandon this approach as soon as they want to. When every student has finished, ask for volunteers to read their poems aloud.

### NOTE

How do we react when confronted with a new object whose use we do not know? What words do we associate with it? What words do we use to define its form or supposed function? This problem is interestingly related to poetry, which usually says something in a new way, thus defining an object, feeling or idea not previously described in this way. This is why in this exercise we use a new or unknown object to stimulate a piece of original writing.

## 1.4

**TIME**
Pre-lesson
homework + 25
minutes in class

**LEVEL**
Higher
elementary +

# OPENERS

Eavesdropping on other people's conversations can be an excellent way of learning a language, particularly when the eavesdropping task is a carefully directed one: for example, 'Listen for the words that follow *I think*' or 'Note down any words you hear when you see people talking and touching'.

In this exercise, eavesdropping is directed to more literary purposes. The aim of the exercise is to raise awareness of literary forms by distinguishing between language that might be an example of a literary form and language that would not.

## Procedure

1 The day before, explain that the first part of this exercise is an out-of-class data collection activity. Ask the students to eavesdrop on as many English conversations as possible and note down any sentences they overhear that would make ideal openings for novels or short stories. These should be brought to class the following day. (Less ambitiously, the sentences can even be collected during the

break period between classes if you are working in a native-speaker environment.)

2 Ask the students to select the best potential opening sentence of a novel or short story from their overheard sentences and to circulate, comparing quotations with each other.

3 Ask the students to form groups with other students who have sentences on the same theme.

4 Ask each group to read their sentences aloud and explain what they have in common.

**VARIATIONS**

1 Tell the students to listen out for possible lines or fragments of a poem. In class, ask the students to work in groups and try to make a whole poem out of their fragments, adding additional material where necessary.

2 Tell the students to note down any striking sentences they overhear. In class, ask the students to work in groups and try to make a short story that uses all these overheard fragments.

**NOTE**

Because it is an eavesdropping activity, this exercise only works well in an environment where spoken English is frequently heard, although if you want to try this in a non-English speaking environment, there is sometimes enough English-language television to make it possible.

ACKNOWLEDGEMENT
We learnt the eavesdropping technique from Gerry Kenny at a Pilgrims teacher training seminar.

# TELLING STORIES

The aim of this exercise is to concentrate the students' attention on the way a story is told. This is an exercise in listening with concentration.

## Preparation

Decide what sort of story you want to work on. Often this will be determined by the subject matter of the text you are reading in class. For example, if you are reading *Shane*, choose a childhood memory of your own associated with a stranger; or if you are about to read the chapter in which Mr Collins proposes to Elizabeth in *Pride and Prejudice*, choose a time when you were surprised by something someone said or did.

## Procedure

1 Ask the students to sit in groups of five or six and ask them to recall a childhood event involving a stranger (assuming we are working with *Shane*). Allow time for each student to recall their event to mind

**1.5**

TIME
20 minutes

LEVEL
Higher
elementary +

SUGGESTED
TEXTS
Any short story

and make sure everyone has done this before going on to the next stage.

2 Tell the groups that they are to follow your instructions exactly. Tell every student to take a turn at describing briefly *only what they saw* and nothing else. When everyone has had their turn, the group should call you over.

3 When you are called over to a group, explain that each student now takes a turn at describing briefly *only the sounds they heard*. Again, the group should call you over when everyone has done this.

4 Finally, each member of the group takes a turn at describing briefly what they felt.

5 When the telling is over, allow the groups time to discuss and explore each other's stories.

### VARIATIONS

1 Ask the students to sit in groups of five or six and ask each member of the group to write down a six-sentence account of the event you are asking them to recall (for example, a childhood memory associated with a stranger). Tell them to number the sentences 1–6. When everyone has written their six sentences, each member of the group takes a turn at reading their first sentence round the circle, then their second, etc. until all six are read.

2 Group the students and ask them to write six sentences as in Variation 1. When everyone has written their six sentences, the group chooses a story-teller who reads their own first sentence aloud. Anyone whose first sentence is at all like it then reads theirs. Next the story-teller reads their second sentence and again anyone with a second sentence at all like it reads theirs. Repeat this procedure with all six sentences, and then choose a second story-teller. Continue until everyone in the group has been story-teller.

### NOTE
If the telling of a story is to a certain extent formalised, the overt formality adds an element that is characteristic of literature. Even an everyday experience related in a formal frame often shows literary qualities. As the text draws attention to (or 'foregrounds') its formal characteristics such as rhyme, rhythm, length of line and sound pattern, the responsibility of the listener or reader to get at the meaning is correspondingly increased. This often makes it more attractive to listen to but more difficult to understand.

ACKNOWLEDGEMENT
This exercise and Variation 1 can be found in Ann Pechou's *The Poet and the Scientists*, Pilgrims Publications 1985.

# RED INDIAN NAMES

**1.6**

**TIME**
30 minutes

**LEVEL**
Higher
elementary +

Perhaps Native Americans find our names exotic; their names (Sitting Bull, Running Deer, Rising Sun) certainly capture our imaginations from early childhood onwards. What aspects of our personality are revealed when we are asked to choose a Native American name for ourselves? This exercise works well as an icebreaker for a new class at the getting to know each other stage. It is also a good way to spend the last half hour of a session.

## Procedure

1 Elicit or explain the meaning of Native American names, how natural images are used to describe the character of a person.
2 Ask the students to sit in a circle. Ask each student to choose a Native American name for themselves and display it on a piece of paper in front of their desks so that their classmates can see it.
3 The rest of the thirty minutes should be used for writing and replying to as many one-line personal questions as students have time to write. Usually the personal question will be inspired by the Native American name, but this is not essential. Each question should be posed in letter form, and the letters should be addressed to and signed with the appropriate Native American names. For example:

Dear Silver Moon,
Does your name mean that you're a night person?
Your friend,
Running Bear

4 Stop the activity after half an hour.

**VARIATIONS**
1 Tell the students that the subject matter of their letters should be a theme or event in a story or novel that the class has been reading. The Native American names help people to be more frank than they might be if they used their own names.
2 This exercise can also be used as a way of discussing a play or a novel. Each member of the class chooses a character from the play or novel as their name and then the students write the one-question letters to each other in character. It does not matter if you have a big class and end up with two of everybody – in fact, it often adds to the interest to get two different replies to the same question.

**NOTE**
The exercise frees the students to ask franker questions and give more honest replies than in face-to-face interaction.

ACKNOWLEDGEMENT
We were first alerted to the possibilities of working with Native American names in an exercise invented by Donna Brandes.

## 1.7

**TIME**
5 minutes per
conversation

**LEVEL**
Higher
elementary +

**SUGGESTED
TEXTS**
Any

# MY TURN, YOUR TURN

It is surprising how fluent a conversation one can have, even when each turn is restricted to a single word. Such conversations can be a valuable summarising exercise for scenes in plays, radio and TV dramas, short stories and chapters in novels.

## Procedure

1 Pair students and instruct them to hold conversations between two literary characters who will be designated by you. Each conversational turn consists of uttering only a single word, and the subject matter of the conversation must relate to what has just been read.
2 Change the characters every two or three minutes or when you see pairs starting to wilt.

### EXAMPLE
For the play-within-the-play scene in *Hamlet*, you might ask for a series of conversations between Hamlet and Claudius, Claudius and Hamlet, Claudius and Polonius, the Player-King and Hamlet, Ophelia and Hamlet, Gertrude and Claudius, etc.

ACKNOWLEDGEMENT
We learnt this technique from Tessa Woodward.

## 1.8

# NAME PAIRS

Understanding the changing nature of language is an important stage for language learners once they have mastered basic linguistic skills. This exercise aims to teach students about context and enable them to think about the implications of class, age and gender in modern English.

## Preparation

Write pairs of names on a series of cards. The names must be varied and should include such pairs as: Albert and Edna; Jason and Sharon; Tarquin and Lucinda; Jake and Victoria; Brian and Sheila; Barney and Gladys; Chuck and Bonny-Lou; Damon and Krystle; William and Alice, etc. Choose names that reflect different classes and ages, also British and American English names. You can use dictionaries of names, or the lists published annually in newspapers of the most popular baptismal names in a given year.

## Procedure

1 Divide the students into groups of three and give each group a prepared card.

**2** Working individually at first, ask the students to spend ten minutes writing down their impressions of the characters, paying special attention to age, social status, nationality (British or American), etc. You may need to discuss with students the significance of names as indicators of class, age, regional background, etc. or you may prefer to let students respond subjectively first and discuss the social dimension later.

**3** After ten minutes, each student passes their card on to the next person and the activity is repeated. After a further ten minutes, the cards are passed on again and the activity is repeated a third time. By this stage, everyone should have short notes on three pairs of names.

**4** Ask everyone to choose one of the three pairs of names and to write a short paragraph describing the characters more fully. The description might include details of what the people look like, what jobs they do, etc.

**5** Ask the students in their groups to share their descriptions with one another and to compare notes on their analysis of the background of their characters.

**6** If time permits, ask the groups to share each other's findings with one another. Allow time for whole-class discussion, when members of the groups can ask questions about the names and hopefully resolve any disagreements which they may have about the social significance of names.

## EXTENSIONS

**1** Ask students to pay special attention to the names of characters in popular fiction. You might bring into the class passages from texts and invite students to change the names and see what the effect is. For example, if Jasper and Lucy are the protagonists of a love story, what is the impact of changing the names to Bob and Ethel? Or if Jim and Sandy are the protagonists of a story about school life, what is the impact of changing their names to Julian and Annabel? This extension is a very effective way of directing students' attention to the signification of naming in the English speaking world.

**2** You can also supply information on the most fashionable names according to lists in birth announcement columns and other figures that are readily available. This extension works well in the multicultural classroom, since it often stimulates a lot of discussion about the power and meaning of names and makes students think more deeply about something they may previously have taken for granted.

## 1.9

**TIME**
30–40 minutes

**LEVEL**
Beginner +

**MATERIALS**
Colour magazines,
scissors, drawing
pins or Blu-tack,
copies of the
chosen text

**SUGGESTED
TEXTS**
Any short poem
around 14–18
lines long

# PICTURE PROMPTING

This exercise aims to help the students to understand a particular text by drawing attention to the difference between the meanings a contemporary reader would find in its vocabulary and those that the writer intended.

## Preparation

Make a vocabulary raid on your chosen poem, selecting up to twelve words. For William Wordsworth's 'Daffodils', for example:

| | | |
|---|---|---|
| cloud | company | crowd |
| dancing | golden | host |
| lake | lonely | pleasure |
| shine | vacant | wealth |

## Procedure

1 Write the words up on the board and make sure the students understand them all.
2 Distribute colour magazines round the class. Ask the students to work in pairs or small groups, finding and cutting out pictures that match the words on the board.
3 When the students have their pictures, read the text out loud and ask them to order the pictures correctly. You will need to read the poem at least three times.
4 Distribute the text. With what different meanings from theirs has the poet used the words? How 'correctly' did they imagine the poem?
5 Ask each group to display all those pictures which have the same connotations as the text on the wall. It is a good idea to display them in the right order and use them as prompts for reciting the poem.

### VARIATION
Where you do not have access to colour magazines, at Step 1 ask the students to work individually and write down several new words they associate with each of the words on the board. When this has been done, read the poem out loud slowly while the students cross out all the words they had written down which were not appropriate. For example, if one of the words they had written down under *wealth* was 'Rolls Royce', this would be inappropriate and should be crossed out.

### NOTE
This exercise focuses on the way in which understanding a text can be difficult because our idea and the writer's idea of what words mean do not always coincide. This is particularly problematical when we are learning a second language and often think each word has only a single meaning.

# REWORKING STORIES

**1.10**

**TIME**
45 minutes

**LEVEL**
Intermediate +

The aim of this exercise is to involve the students in a very conscious way in the composition process in story writing.

## Procedure

1 Ask the students to sit in groups of five or six. Ask each student to think of a story from their own culture or childhood – folk tales, fairy tales, nursery stories are all fine. Allow up to three minutes for this.
2 Each student takes a turn at telling their story to other members of the group. No story should take longer than three minutes.
3 Ask each student to choose one of the stories they have heard and write their own *altered* version of it. Each student must decide in what way to alter it, by changing the setting, making it autobiographical, turning it into a political satire, etc.
4 Once everyone has written their altered version, display them on the walls. The students circulate, reading them and taking down and collecting any that they recognise as altered versions of their own originals.

### VARIATIONS

1 At Step 3, ask the students to introduce an additional character into their story – themselves, a politician, a 'soap' character, etc.
2 It is also possible to do this exercise as a whole-class activity. At Step 2, ask for five or six volunteers to tell their stories to the whole class. At Step 3, one option is to ask students to write in pairs rather than individually. And at Step 4, you can also ask the writers to return their reworked stories directly to the story-teller; this allows small groups to form around each story-teller to read the several different versions of the same story.

# RETELLING STORIES

**1.11**

**TIME**
60 minutes

**LEVEL**
Intermediate +

This exercise involves listening comprehension and also tests the way in which individual students can assimilate material. Its aim is to draw attention to the ways in which we listen and how we hear only what seems most relevant to us.

## Procedure

1 Divide the students into groups of three. It is best if the groups find a place for themselves somewhere in the room, not necessarily sitting at desks, because in the first stages this exercise is very noisy and each group needs its own corner in which to work.
2 Tell each group to appoint a 'story-teller', a 'listener' and a 'documenter'. The documenter has paper and a pen and should

write notes. The story-teller tells the other two in the group a simple fairy tale, myth or folk tale, such as the story of Cinderella or the story of Icarus' flight to the sun or something along those lines. The listener does nothing but listen while the documenter takes notes. Tell the students they have three minutes to recount their story.

3 At the end of three minutes, the listener has to tell the same story back to the original teller, taking a further three minutes in which to do it. The documenter now makes notes about this second version of the story.

4 Finally, the documenter gives both story-teller and listener their version of their two accounts of the same tale. There are often massive discrepancies between the versions that the other two students might not have seen at all.

5 The members of the group then change roles and the process is repeated.

6 Finally, they change roles again for the third and last time, so each student has a chance to be story-teller, listener and documenter.

7 If time permits, there can be a general discussion of what has taken place in each group.

### EXTENSION

The following extension often produces surprising results, because frequently the most obvious, elementary details of the stories are omitted by one or other of the speakers. Often additional details are included when the listener gives the second version, and so the role of the documenter is a crucial one since only he or she can pinpoint these distinctions.

Each person tries to write two versions of a story, taking into account the differences that the third person has pointed out. You can also use this extension as a way of introducing the class to the question of point of view in narrative.

Writers who are especially useful for discussing point of view as it emerges in narrative are Henry James and D H Lawrence.

## 1.12

**TIME**
15 minutes

**LEVEL**
Intermediate +

**SUGGESTED TEXTS**
Short stories

## MIRRORING STORIES

The aim of this exercise is to heighten the impact of a story by increasing the responsibility of the listeners and by ritualising the telling.

## Preparation

Either you or the student story-teller must be able to tell a 3–5 minute story (either from literature or experience) with reasonable fluency. If you are using this technique with a class for the first time, it is best to take the story-teller's role yourself and to prepare the story you are going to tell fairly carefully.

# Procedure

1 Arrange the chairs so that the students sit in a circle that is very nearly complete. If this cannot be done, the exercise will not work. The story-teller sits in the centre of the circle facing the place where the circle is not complete (see Fig. 1). He or she asks for two volunteers to come and listen to the story. They should sit directly facing the story-teller with their chairs touching. Their knees must be 25–30 centimetres from the story-teller's.

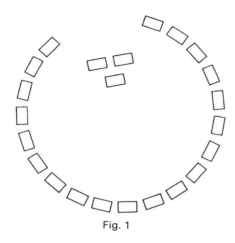

Fig. 1

2 Explain that the following is going to happen:
   i The story-teller is going to tell the story to the two listeners, not to the whole group.
   ii When the story is complete, the two listeners will tell it back again to the story-teller. They should try to use exactly the same words as the original teller. They may help each other and take turns at retelling the story.
   iii When the listeners have retold, or 'mirrored', the story, any 'bystander' in the outer circle who can add or correct a detail may do so. To do this, a bystander must get up, walk round the outside of the circle, enter the circle through the gap, and go and crouch beside/between the two listeners before adding or correcting the detail. This done, the bystander returns to his or her seat by the same route. The routine is absolutely sacrosanct and may not be varied in any way. If you act as story-teller when this exercise is first practised, you can ensure by quiet guidance that all the procedures are followed.

NOTE
This exercise is based on techniques that are borrowed from psychodrama. This is a form of therapy in which an individual's hurtful

experience is reenacted in a drama involving other members of the therapy group. One of the techniques used in psychodrama is 'mirroring'. This technique allows an individual to discover the effects on others of what they say by having someone say it to them in the course of the drama. This idea of mirroring has a very obvious application in the quite different context of language learning where both exact repetition and paraphrase are useful activities. In this exercise the technique is used in a formal way reminiscent of some forms of mirroring used in psychodrama.

## 1.13

**TIME**
Stage 1:
30 minutes
Stage 2:
25 minutes
Stage 3:
20 minutes

**LEVEL**
Intermediate +

# GENDER PRONOUNS

The aim of this exercise is to raise students' awareness of the question of gender in a text.

## Procedure

STAGE 1
Hand out copies of a text, which must contain references to 'he' and 'she'. The text given here is a passage from Edith Wharton's novel, *The Age of Innocence*, first published in 1920.

Did she really imagine that he and she could live like this? And if not, what else did she imagine?
  'Tomorrow I must see you – somewhere where we can be alone,' he said, in a voice that sounded almost angry to his own ears.
She wavered and moved towards the carriage.
  'But I shall be at Granny's – for the present that is,' she added, as if conscious that her change of plans required some explanation.
  'Somewhere where we can be alone,' he insisted.
She gave a faint laugh that grated on him.
  'In New York? But there are no churches,... no monuments.'
  'There's the Art Museum - in the Park,' he explained, as she looked puzzled.
  'At half past two. I shall be at the door...'
  She turned away without answering and got quickly into the carriage. As it drove off she leaned forward, and he thought she waved her hand in the obscurity. He started after her in a turmoil of contradictory feelings.

Ask the students to rewrite the pronouns in the text with pronouns of the opposite gender. So all the 'she' pronouns are replaced with 'he' and vice versa. The class then divides into groups of three or four and each group has five minutes in which to decide on the basic differences for a reader that arise from a substitution of pronouns in this way. At the end of five minutes, each group reports back to the whole class and the students compare what they have done.
  This first stage of the exercise usually reveals significant differences,

but students may sometimes have difficulty in articulating what those differences are. In the above passage, if it is 'she' and not 'he' who is insisting on the meeting tomorrow, then the tone of the passage may seem to change and the character may appear to be nagging rather than persuading. Likewise, a 'he' who says he is going to be at his Granny's next day will sound slightly silly to English ears. Ask students to note the points in the text where they think substitution of pronouns will make little or no difference at all.

## STAGE 2
Split the group into pairs and ask each person to write three sentences, but to leave blank the gender pronoun. When everyone has written the three sentences, each pair exchanges papers and each fills in the blanks in the other's sentences with a 'he' or a 'she'. At the end of this stage, all the pairs exchange notes on their decisions.

## STAGE 3
The final stage of the activity involves the invention of a new, non-gender-specific pronoun. You can choose to introduce the class to examples of this kind of writing, either by extracts from Marge Piercy's *Woman on the Edge of Time*, or Ursula Le Guin's *The Left Hand of Darkness*, or you can leave this to the end of the class after everyone has tried to create a new pronoun individually.

Ask the students to write a sentence in which the gender of the subject is left unspecified. In place of *he* or *she*, they invent a completely new term ('e' for example). At the end of this stage, the class compares their inventions.

## NOTE
This exercise can produce quite surprising results, and sometimes the inventions are very sophisticated. It is a good discussion activity, and is also useful in introducing students to the ongoing debates about language and gender, especially since many will have been taught that the pronoun *he* in English is acceptable as a neutral, all-embracing word. You can introduce elements of the history of language into this class too, and can discuss with students the differences between languages with grammatical gender and those without.

## 1.14

**TIME**
3 minutes

**LEVEL**
Beginner +

# BREAKING THE MOOD

It is not always easy to move from one activity or text to another. This is a satisfying, fun way of leaving a literary text behind.

## Procedure

Ask each student to choose any three or four consecutive words from the text the class has just been reading. At a given signal, all the students start repeating their phrases simultaneously. You can orchestrate the noise level (and when you get good at it, even the vowel quantities and the tempo) by 'conducting' the class. Allow it to continue for up to a minute.

### VARIATION
You can also use gibberish as a moodbreaker. Each student maintains a continuous gibberish version of the way a character in the play, story or novel speaks.

## 1.15

**TIME**
At least 30 minutes

**LEVEL**
Intermediate +

**MATERIALS**
Each word of your chosen text written on a separate piece of paper

**CLASS SIZE**
Ideally 11–20. Larger classes must be divided into groups of this size

**SUGGESTED TEXTS**
One or two lines of poetry

# JIGSAW LINES

The aim of the exercise is to make stylistic judgments about alternative orderings of a set of words.

The line or couplet you work with can be part of a large text you are going to work on subsequently or it can be chosen for its thematic relevance to the class's ongoing work.

## Preparation

Choose a single line or couplet with exactly as many words as there are students in the class. Write each word on a separate small piece of paper. If class attendance is unpredictable, prepare two or three lines of different lengths so that there will always be one line available with exactly the right number of words.

## Procedure

1  Place the pieces of paper word-side downwards and ask each student to take one.
2  Tell the students to make as many copies of their word as there are other members of the class. Each copy should be on a separate small piece of paper.
3  Tell the students to circulate, exchanging one of their words for one of each of their classmates'. When students give each other words, they should accompany the gift with an explanation of why it is being given – for example, 'Mauro, I'm giving you this word because if you ever knock at mine, it'll always be opened to you,' as you give him a piece of paper with the word *door* written on it.
4  Once each student has collected a word from every other student,

they should settle down individually and try to reconstitute the original line from the words they have been given and their own original word.

**5** When students think they are getting somewhere, they can discuss their progress with colleagues. Alternatively, instruct the students to display their lines on their desks and circulate reading colleagues' suggested versions.

## SUGGESTED TEXTS
The following texts work well:

*10 words*
- To a mind that is still the whole universe surrenders
  Lao Tse, *Tao-te-ching*
- It (water) rests content in those lowly places which others despise
  *ibid*

*11 words*
- The earth doth like a snake renew her winter weeds outworn
  Shelley, 'Hellas'

*12 words*
- Our noisy years seem moments in the being of the eternal silence
  William Wordsworth, 'Ode on Intimations of Immortality'
- She bid me take love easy as the leaves grow on the tree
  W B Yeats, 'Down by the Salley Gardens'

*13 words*
- Men might rise on stepping stones of their own selves to higher things
  Alfred Tennyson, 'In Memoriam'
- Who cares if some one-eyed son-of-a-bitch invents an instrument to measure Spring with
  e e cummings, 'Sonnet'
- To all the dictators who look so bold and fresh / The midnight hours
  W H Auden and Louis MacNeice, 'Last Will and Testament'

*14 words*
- Ask me no more where Jove bestows when June is past the fading rose
  Thomas Carew, 'Ask Me No More'

*15 words*
- And suddenly one more impatient cried / Who is the potter pray and who the pot
  Edward Fitzgerald's translation of *The Rubaiyat of Omar Khayyam*

*16 words*
- The voice I hear this passing night was heard in ancient days by emperor and clown
  John Keats, 'Ode to a Nightingale'
- Bliss was it in that dawn to be alive / And to be young was very heaven
  William Wordsworth, *The Prelude*

*17 words*
- So passeth in the passing of a day / Of mortal life the leaf the bud the flower
  Edmund Spenser, *The Faerie Queene*

*18 words*
- We are such stuff as dreams are made on and our little life is rounded with a sleep
  William Shakespeare, *The Tempest*

*19 words*
- The sky is darkening like a stain / Something is going to fall like rain / And it won't be flowers
  W H Auden and Christopher Isherwood, *The Dog Beneath the Skin*

*20 words*
- And not till the Goths again come running down from the hill / Will cease the clangour of the electric drill
  Louis MacNeice, 'Eclogue for Christmas'

**NOTE**

In this exercise students are challenged to puzzle out the best possible order for a set of words that together make an aesthetic and linguistic whole. Putting together the pieces of a jigsaw is not a new idea, but it works especially well for literature since the sum of the parts is a considerable text. Almost all the end results are pleasing although they are rarely 'right'. Most students tackle this task by grouping the separate words into three or four larger constituents and then making stylistic judgments about the most satisfying order for these larger constituents.

## 1.16

**TIME**
40 minutes

**LEVEL**
Intermediate +

**MATERIALS**
Handouts of a poem in its original version and also typed without line breaks or punctuation

**SUGGESTED TEXTS**
Any short poem (14–30 lines)

# RESHAPING POEMS

This exercise involves the students in making decisions about line boundaries and punctuation and in experimenting with the different effects that different decisions bring about. The aim is to raise awareness of the options and the criteria at work in this important area of composition.

## Preparation

Prepare a text by typing it continuously without line breaks or punctuation and make a copy for each student. Alternatively, write it up in this form on the board.

So Ted Hughes's poem 'Hawk Roosting' would look like this:

I sit in the top of the wood my eyes closed inaction no falsifying dream between my hooked head and hooked feet or in sleep rehearse perfect kills and eat the convenience of the high trees the air's buoyancy and the sun's ray are of advantage to me and the earth's face upward for my inspection my feet are locked upon the rough bark it took the whole of Creation to produce my foot my each feather now I hold Creation in my foot or fly up and revolve it all slowly I kill where I please because it is all mine there is no sophistry in my body my manners are tearing off heads the allotment of death for the one path of my flight is direct through the bones of the living no arguments assert my right the sun is behind me nothing has changed since I began my eye has permitted no change I am going to keep things like this

## Procedure

1 Ask the students to work in groups of five or six.
2 Hand out one copy of the prepared text to each group.
3 Working as a group, the students make decisions about where to put the line boundaries and then write the text out in lines, fully punctuated.
4 Allow time for the various versions to be circulated or displayed on the wall. Explain that each group should make any changes to their own text which are inspired by the work of other groups.
5 Hand out or display copies of the original unadulterated poem (see below) and ask the students to compare their versions with it.

HAWK ROOSTING

I sit in the top of the wood, my eyes closed.
Inaction, no falsifying dream
Between my hooked head and hooked feet:
Or in sleep rehearse perfect kills and eat.

The convenience of the high trees!
The air's buoyancy and the sun's ray
Are of advantage to me;
And the earth's face upward for my inspection.

My feet are locked upon the rough bark.
It took the whole of Creation
To produce my foot, my each feather:
Now I hold Creation in my foot

Or fly up, and revolve it all slowly —
I kill where I please because it is all mine.
There is no sophistry in my body:
My manners are tearing off heads —

The allotment of death.
For the one path of my flight is direct
Through the bones of the living.
No arguments assert my right:

The sun is behind me.
Nothing has changed since I began.
My eye has permitted no change.
I am going to keep things like this.

Ted Hughes

**VARIATIONS**

1 This technique also works well for pop music. The students listen to the song while marking the beginning and end of sense groups in a continuously typed text. With some songs, deciding how to set them out on a page so that the harmonic variety is captured is also an intriguing exercise.

2 Get the students to suggest improvements to an original text by inserting the line boundaries in different places from those of the poet. This also works well for 'Hawk Roosting'. For more advanced students, this idea can be combined with inserting additional words, particularly rhymes.

## 1.17

**TIME**
10 minutes

**LEVEL**
Intermediate +

**MATERIALS**
Copies of text

# THE FIRST MEN ON MERCURY

If every attempt to understand literature results in a paraphrase that takes us one step further away from the original text, there must be strong arguments for reading a text and resisting the temptation to analyse and explain it in detail. This is easiest to do when you have a text whose impact is obvious and which delights more on first reading than when explained in detail. A text that lends itself perfectly to this approach is Edwin Morgan's poem 'The First Men on Mercury'. The best time for this exercise is the last ten minutes of a lesson.

## Procedure

1 Divide the class into two halves. Try to avoid the 'All those sitting on my right...' approach. Also avoid dividing by sex, age, etc. If you are a spectacle-wearer yourself, those who wear glasses and those who do not is a good way to divide. Although divided into two halves, the class should remain sitting in their original places.

2 Explain that the poem will be read aloud with each half of the class taking turns at reading a verse and that you will lead the half of the class that takes the even-numbered verses.

THE FIRST MEN ON MERCURY

– We come in peace from the third planet.
  Would you take us to your leader?
– BAWR STRETTER! BAWR. BAWR. STRETTERHAWL?
– This is a little plastic model
  of the solar system, with working parts.
  You are here and we are there and we
  are now here with you, is this clear?

   — GAWL HORROP. BAWR. ABAWRHANNAHANNA!
   — Where we come from is blue and white
      with brown, you see we call the brown
      here 'land', and the blue is 'sea', and the white
      is 'clouds' over land and sea, we live
      on the surface of the brown land,
      all round is sea and clouds. We are 'men'.
      Men come —
   — GLAWP MEN! GAWRBENNER MENKO. MENHAWL?
   — Men come in peace from the third planet
      which we call 'earth'. We are earthmen.
      Take us earthmen to your leader.
   — THMEN? THMEN? BAWR. BAWRHOSSOP.
      YULEEDA TAN HANNA. HARRABOST YULEEDA.
   — I am the yuleeda. You see my hands.
      we can carry no benner, we come in peace.
      The spaceways are all stretterhawn.
   — GLAWN PEACEMEN ALL HORRABHANNA TANTKO!
      TAN COME AT'MSTROSSOP. GLAWP YULEEDA!
   — Atoms are peacegawl in our harraban.
      Menbat worrabost from tan hannahanna.
   — YOU MEN WE KNOW BAWRHOSSOPTANT. BAWR.
      WE KNOW YULEEDA. GO STRAWG BACKSPETTER QUICK.
   — We cantantabawr, tantingko backspetter now!
   — BANGHAPPER NOW! YES, THIRD PLANET BACK.
      YULEEDA WILL GO BACK BLUE, WHITE, BROWN
      NOWHANNA! THERE IS NO MORE TALK.
   — Gawl han fasthapper?
   — NO. YOU MUST GO BACK TO YOUR PLANET.
      GO BACK IN PEACE, TAKE WHAT YOU HAVE GAINED
      BUT QUICKLY.
   — Stretterworra gawl, gawl...
   — OF COURSE, BUT NOTHING IS EVER THE SAME,
      NOW IS IT? YOU'LL REMEMBER MERCURY.

Edwin Morgan

# CHAPTER 2

# *One text*

This chapter contains sixteen exercises based on a single text, 'I remember, I remember' by Thomas Hood (1799-1845). Virtually all the exercises can also be used with a wide range of texts.

We decided to set aside a whole chapter for exercises based on a single text because we wanted to illustrate the many different ways there are of working with a text and that there is not a single right approach. We hope this example will encourage you to experiment with a variety of approaches to the texts you know well.

We chose 'I remember, I remember' because it relates universal personal experiences, and focuses on memory and the passing of time. It also conveys a strong sense of location and relates to the learner's personal experience outside the classroom. These are all obvious advantages and show that thematic criteria are important in choosing texts to work with.

At the end of this chapter (page 49) you will find three more poems about memory, which you may also like to work with. Meanwhile, here is 'I remember, I remember':

> **I REMEMBER, I REMEMBER**
>
> I remember, I remember
> The house where I was born,
> The little window where the sun
> Came peeping in at morn;
> 5    He never came a wink too soon,
> Nor brought too long a day;
> But now, I often wish the night
> Had borne my breath away!
>
> I remember, I remember
> 10   The roses, red and white,
> The violets, and the lily-cups,
> Those flowers made of light!
> The lilacs where the robin built,
> And where my brother set
> 15   The laburnum on his birthday, —
> The tree is living yet!

I remember, I remember
Where I was used to swing,
And thought the air must rush as fresh
20   To swallows on the wing;
My spirit flew in feathers then,
That is so heavy now,
And summer pools could hardly cool
The fever on my brow!

25   I remember, I remember
The fir trees dark and high;
I used to think their slender tops
Were close against the sky:
It was a childish ignorance,
30   But now 'tis little joy
To know I'm farther off from heav'n
Than when I was a boy.

Thomas Hood

# PREDICTING

This exercise can be used for poems or short stories; its aim is to establish the subject matter and type of the text in the minds of the students before they read it. This facilitates reading with understanding by providing the necessary schema in advance.

## Procedure

1 Write on the board a few key words from the text the class is going to read. For verse 1 of 'I remember, I remember' for example, *house, window, sun, night,* and *breath.*
2 Group the students in threes and give them fifteen minutes to write a twenty-five word version of the text they are going to read. Their versions must include the five words on the board and must be *exactly* twenty-five words long.
3 Ask groups to read their versions aloud before you read the authentic text.

**VARIATION**
At Step 1 you can present the key words in the order in which they occur in the text (as here) or in alphabetical order. Alphabetical order usually works best with short stories, which typically require 8–12 key words.

**NOTE**
With longer word lists you can also allow up to forty word versions of the text to be read; it is best always to set an exact number. The word

**2.1**

**TIME**
25 minutes

**LEVEL**
Elementary +

**SUGGESTED TEXTS**
Any poem or short story

limit should be four or five times the number of key words you write up on the board.

ACKNOWLEDGEMENT
This is a cousin of 'What's in the Text' in John Morgan and Mario Rinvolucri's *Vocabulary*, OUP 1986, pp 12–13.

## 2.2

**TIME**
20–25 minutes

**LEVEL**
Elementary +

**CLASS SIZE**
Larger classes

# GROUPING

Most of us sometimes and some of us usually tell students who they are to work with in small groups: 'You, you and you' (pointing) or 'You two by the window' are too commonly part of our repertoires. When groups form, there may be many more interesting things their members have in common than that they happen to be sitting by the window. Good teachers will be on the lookout for ways of grouping students that are interesting and natural.

In this grouping exercise, we have used the theme of memories because it relates to 'I remember, I remember'. Any theme which relates to the text the class are reading works equally well.

## Procedure

1 Ask the students to sit in silence for between three and five minutes, preferably with their eyes shut, while they recall a childhood memory.
2 Tell the students to form groups according to whether the memory is a morning, afternoon or night-time one.
3 If a group is still too big, subdivide by early/late morning/afternoon or evening/night.
4 If required, further subdivisions are possible:
   • Is the memory principally associated with sight, sound, touch, taste or smell?
   • Is it an indoor or an outdoor memory?
   • Is it a spring, summer, autumn or winter memory?
5 Allow the groups a few minutes while the members exchange their common memories before you start to work with them.

**VARIATION**
If you want to pair students, follow Step 1, and then ask them to categorise their memories on a sheet of paper according to the following criteria:
• Morning, afternoon, night time
• Sight, sound, touch, taste, smell
• Indoors, outdoors
• Spring, summer, autumn, winter.
The students then circulate, holding up their papers and trying to find a partner with whom they have two or three common categories.

# EXCHANGING

**2.3**

**TIME**
Up to 1 hour

**LEVEL**
Higher
elementary +

**MATERIALS**
A language labora-
tory which allows
students to record
their own material

**SUGGESTED
TEXTS**
Short poems or
short, short
stories

The aim of this exercise is to show how the language laboratory can be used for an exercise based on a literary text.

## Preparation

Set the lab up with a blank cassette in each recorder.

## Procedure

1 Tell each student to record the following statement: ' Please listen carefully to my memory and to anything which anyone else has recorded after it before you record your response.'
2 Distribute copies of 'I remember, I remember' for each student to read silently. Tell the students to record any memory which the text sparks off.
3 The students then circulate, listening to each others' recorded memories and adding any further new memories or comments of their own. Allow at least thirty minutes for this stage.
4 The students return to their own cassette recorders and listen to what others have added to their cassettes.

**NOTE**
In *Bring the Language Lab Back to Life*, Philip Ely suggests many excit-ing, person-related ways of working with the language lab. His approach can easily be extended to working with literature, as we have tried to show here.

# ASSESSING

**2.4**

**TIME**
30 minutes

**LEVEL**
Higher
elementary –
Intermediate+

**SUGGESTED
TEXTS**
Poems, short
stories, novels

This exercise asks the students to make some decisions about the writer. These may be taken intuitively or be supported by evidence, but in either case the students will be obliged to understand and assimilate the text in order to answer the questions. The aim of the exercise is also partly to create the feeling that the writer is, like ourselves, a real person with a distinct character and their own strengths and weaknesses. The exercise can only be done after the poem has been read.

## Procedure

1 The class makes a long list of social skills, such as entertaining, shutting up bores, putting people at their ease, and getting others to agree. Write these skills up on the board as they are brainstormed and continue until you have at least twenty.
2 Working in small groups, the class decides which of these social skills Thomas Hood would be good at and which he would not.

**VARIATIONS**

There are endless variations on this very rich theme:

1 In small groups the students can make questionnaires on virtually any topic for other groups to answer in the persona of the writer.

2 An individual student can take on the persona of the writer and the rest of the class can interview them.

3 If the class is doing a vocabulary exercise which involves sharing lists of nouns (for example, objects they can see around them), someone can be the writer and after each item say whether they would want it in their home. There can be two or three different writers (e.g. 'Christina Rossetti', 'Jane Austen', 'William Wordsworth') making judgments for each item.

4 The class can imagine questions the writer might want to ask them.

## 2.5

**TIME**
Stage 1:
30 minutes
Stage 2 (optional):
30 minutes

**LEVEL**
Elementary +

**MATERIALS**
Text of poem

**SUGGESTED TEXTS**
6–8 lines of simple poetry

# TRANSLATING

Members of the Deaf community communicate in Sign Language by using their hands, faces and bodies to convey meaning. In Britain the language of the Deaf community, BSL or British Sign Language, has an entirely different grammatical structure from spoken English. Any hearing person who has ever seen a Sign Language poem recited (together with an accompanying interpretation) will have been fascinated trying to work out which elements of Sign Language are not only meaningful but also poetic. Equally interesting is the problem of trying to translate an English text into first Sign Language and then Sign poetry.

## Procedure

STAGE 1

1 Group the students in fours and distribute one copy of the first verse of 'I remember, I remember' to each group.

2 Tell the students they have twenty minutes to work out a Sign version of the text and that each group's version must be performed simultaneously by all four members of the group.

3 At the end of the twenty minutes, each group should perform. You can encourage applause for good performances – but in BSL of course: raise both arms above the head and with fingers slightly spread move each hand by rapid twisting movements of the wrist.

STAGE 2 (optional): Making a Sign poem

1 Working as a whole class, ask the students to choose the best version of each line or couplet from those already invented.

2 Ask the class to make suggestions as to how this Sign text could be made more poetic. You will need to explain that a Sign poem is a poem in three-dimensional space and that poetic effects in Sign Language are achieved by the way the hands (and body) move in this space.

ACKNOWLEDGEMENT
David Brien of the Deaf Studies Unit at the University of Durham and Clark Denmark of the British Deaf Association supplemented our inadequate knowledge of and about BSL.

# EXEMPLIFYING

**2.6**

**TIME**
30–40 minutes

**LEVEL**
Intermediate +

**MATERIALS**
Blu-tack or drawing pins

**SUGGESTED TEXTS**
Any short poem with a structure whose development is marked by words like *If...* *then...* and *Once... now... when...,* etc.

The aim of the exercise is to draw attention to the way the writer connects ideas so that the meaning of the text as a whole is clear because the structure of the argument is understood.

As soon as we hear or read the word *if*, we know there are two parts to the sentence. Very often in a piece of writing, it is possible to identify the words like *if, so* and *because* that connect one idea to another. Once we understand the way the various parts of a text are connected, we are more likely to understand the text as a whole. In this exercise, students describe their own experience within the same connecting framework as that of the poem they are about to read.

## Procedure

1 Write the connecting framework of the last verse of 'I remember, I remember' up on the board like this:

I remember. . .
I used to think . . .
It was a childish ignorance, but now . . .

Ask the students to copy it down and fill in the gaps in a way that would be true for a past experience of their own. Allow ten to fifteen minutes for relatively simple outlines like this one and fifteen to twenty-five minutes for more complex ones.
2 As they finish, the students form small groups and share their work. Later the texts can be displayed on the wall.

## 2.7

**TIME**
45 minutes

**LEVEL**
Elementary +

**MATERIALS**
Blu-tack or
drawing pins

**SUGGESTED
TEXTS**
Any short poem

# VISUALISING

Asking students to visualise a past experience is a very powerful technique for enabling them to recall memories. These can be used as an aid to understanding a text by matching it with their memories. Reading or hearing a poem then becomes a task reading or task listening exercise.

## Procedure

1  Tell the students you are going to ask them to recall to memory something from their past experience. The particular topic you choose will be suggested by the central images of the poem – for example, a spring walk in the country if your text is William Wordsworth's 'Daffodils', or memories of the house (and garden) of their childhood for 'I remember, I remember'.

2  They should first find a relaxed position (even lying on the floor if that is possible), loosen tight clothing and, most important, *close their eyes.*

3  Explain that only you will break the silence and that after you have spoken four times, the silence will continue for a while.

4  Take the students back into their past by making four or five simple, memory awakening statements. It is important to speak slowly, softly and in a relaxing voice. Pause for twenty seconds between statements. For 'I remember, I remember' the statements might be:

   • It's early morning: you are lying in the bed you slept in when you were very young. (*15-20 second pause*)
   • Allow the sights and sounds to come back to you one by one. (*pause*)
   • You may be aware of what's going on outside the room, in the garden or in the street.(*pause*)
   • How will you spend your day? Continue to relive your childhood.

5  When you judge the time is right, probably after a further two or three minutes, bring the class slowly back to the present by interrupting the relaxation in a low voice, saying something like: 'When you open your eyes, open them slowly; look around – slowly.' Then allow time. 'As you sit up, will you take a sheet of paper and divide it into eight or ten separate small pieces – there's no hurry.'

6  When the students have divided their sheets of paper, ask them to write eight or ten different images from their visualisation on the pieces of paper (one on each).

7  Present the poem by whatever technique you are using (for example, by reading it aloud or playing a recording).

8  Ask each student to divide their pieces of paper into three categories: images that coincide with those in the poem, images that are tenuously related, and images that do not coincide at all. Read the poem again while students check the categorisations.

9  Designate three walls, one for images that coincide (Wall 1), one for

tenuously related images (Wall 2 – to the right of Wall 1), one for those that do not coincide (Wall 3 – to the right of Wall 2). Ask the students to display their pieces of paper on the appropriate wall.

10 Divide the class into three groups and allocate one group to each wall. There are two possible continuations from here:

    **a** Each group tries to categorise the pieces of paper on their wall according to whatever criteria seem appropriate. After ten or fifteen minutes, ask each group to explain their rationale to the other two groups;

    **b** Each group orders the pieces of paper on their wall from those most connected to the poem (displayed on the left-hand end of the wall) to those least connected to the poem (displayed on the right-hand end of the wall). When this has been done, allow time for everyone to move round reading the pieces of paper.

**NOTES**

1 If you follow Step 10b, you will end up with a wall display which shows the extent to which the world of the poet and the world of the class match each other. It is often very instructive to see in display form the extent to which we share a common culture with a figure from the past.

2 If you have not tried visualisation before, you may be apprehensive about how your students will react and about whether you will do it well. But once you have tried it, visualisation becomes easier and more natural for you and the students each time you repeat it.

# ASSOCIATING

This exercise is comparable to the following one in assuming that if the students can relate to the subject matter of the text, they can understand its meaning. It involves crossing out anything which is not part of their own experience (cf. Exercise 7.7 *Words that fit*) and leaving behind only those parts of the text to which they truly relate. The aim of the exercise is to help the students to be aware of reacting in different ways to different parts of the text.

## Procedure

1 Working individually, each student tries to associate with each line of the poem. Have they ever had a similar experience? Any line they cannot associate with or relate to in this way should be crossed out.

2 The poem should then be read chorally: the students only read those lines they have not crossed out.

**VARIATION**

With smaller classes, instead of a choral reading, each learner reads their surviving text aloud in turn.

**2.8**

**TIME**
20–25 minutes

**LEVEL**
Higher
elementary +

**MATERIALS**
A copy of the text
that can be
written on

**SUGGESTED
TEXTS**
Any short poem

## 2.9

**TIME**
40–60 minutes
(depending on
class size)

**LEVEL**
Higher
elementary +

**SUGGESTED
TEXTS**
Any short poem

# MEANING

Like Exercise 2.8 *Associating*, the aim of this exercise is to promote the ability to discriminate between the effect on us of one part of the text and another.

## Procedure

1 Ask the students to work through 'I remember, I remember', deciding whether to associate each line with sight, sound, taste, touch or smell. Ask them to decide on one main sense for each line.

2 Divide the class into five groups. Each group takes one of the senses and tries to find out how many other students in the class associated each of the lines with this sense. If time allows, each group can make a bar chart or graph displaying the information they have discovered about their sense.

3 Read the poem aloud. Ask the students to close their eyes and try to experience the sense they associated with each line as you read. Alternatively, ask the students to mime the ways in which they would experience the sense they associated with each line as you read. You may need to read the poem aloud a second time for a more polished performance.

### VARIATIONS

1 A more teacher-dominated variation at Step 2 is to collate the information on the board. This shortens the time required, but deprives the students of the communicative part of the exercise.

2 With larger classes, a possible variation at Step 3 is to have each group contribute the lines predominantly associated with their sense in a whole-class choral reading of the poem. (This means that first the class has to agree which lines are predominantly associated with which sense.)

3 Other areas one can work with besides the five senses include thought/feeling; sadness/happiness; childhood/adulthood/old age; feelings – good/bad/neutral.

### NOTE

How do we know what sentences mean? Even linguists are uncertain about how to answer this question and usually fall back on saying that if we know whether the sentence is true or false, we know what it means. (This is the theory known as 'Truth-conditional Semantics'.) This exercise is based on the proposition that if we can associate a sentence with one of the five senses, then we know what it means.

# CONTRIBUTING

It is immensely easier for students to understand the poem they are reading when they write part of it themselves. This exercise centres on a technique that allows each student to make a contribution to the poem being read.

## Preparation

You will need to make sure you have a suitable text for this exercise, that it is properly prepared and a copy made for each student. We exemplify the exercise at intermediate level with 'I remember, I remember', prepared so that it looks like this:

Verse 1 I remember, I remember
(Group 1)
But now, I often wish the night
Had borne my breath away!

Verse 2 I remember, I remember
(Group 2)
And where my brother set
The laburnum on his birthday,
The tree is living yet!

Verse 3 I remember, I remember
(Group 3)
My spirit flew in feathers then,
That is so heavy now,
And summer pools could hardly cool
The fever on my brow!

Verse 4 I remember, I remember
(Group 4)
It was a childish ignorance,
But now 'tis little joy
To know I'm farther off from heav'n
Than when I was a boy.

You can save time by photocopying the text above. (But remember that you can only do this with texts that are out of copyright, i.e. where the writer has been dead for at least fifty years.)

## Procedure

1 Ask each student to write down a childhood memory they recall with pleasure. They should write a short phrase. For groups smaller than twenty, two memories per student work best.
2 Divide the class into four groups, and distribute the prepared handout. The class reads the poem in the following way:

**TIME**
30 minutes

**LEVEL**
Higher elementary – Advanced, depending on the difficulty of the text selected

**MATERIALS**
A class set of specially typed handouts of a poem

**SUGGESTED TEXTS**
See Suggested Texts below

i Thomas Hood's text is read chorally by the whole class

ii The gap in Verse 1 is filled by Group 1, with each student reading their memory/ies aloud in turn; the gap in Verse 2 is filled by Group 2, with each student reading their memory/ies aloud; etc.

3 The authentic text should then be read chorally again but with each group reading the original words in the verse they contributed to.

**SUGGESTED TEXTS**

Other texts that work well treated in this way include:

• For elementary-level students, Eleanor Farjeon's 'Cats'. Remove from 'Any table...' to '...With your frocks'. Ask the students to suggest places a cat might sleep in as their contribution to the text.

• For intermediate-level students, Coventry Patmore's 'The Toys'. Remove from 'A box of counters...' to '...with careful art'. Ask the students to suggest small objects that kept them company or had sentimental value for them when they were children as their contribution to the text.

• For really advanced-level students, Rupert Brooke's 'The Great Lover'. Remove from 'White plates...' to '...last year's ferns'. Ask the students to suggest the things that make people feel it is good to be alive.

**VARIATION**

A large board to write the text on or an OHP transparency and overlay can substitute for a handout.

ACKNOWLEDGEMENT

This idea is Barry Palmer's and is to be found in *The Literary Practice Handbook*, University of East Anglia, 1984, p 16.

## 2.11

**TIME**
20 minutes

**LEVEL**
Higher
elementary +

**MATERIALS**
Correction fluid, a
copy of the text
that can be
written on

**SUGGESTED
TEXTS**
Short poems

# CLOZING

In this exercise the students are asked to supply items that have been removed from a text and that belong to a common grammatical category. This is a good exercise because the students learn something grammatical (for example, where adverbs are placed) through focusing on the semantic possibilities (which words would make sense in the given context). And it works better in poetry where more careful judgments are required since prosody, i.e. rhyme and rhythm, as well as the meaning, affects possible choices. The exercise therefore aims to have the students make judgments at several linguistic levels – syntactic, semantic and phonological.

## Preparation

White out all the words in a given syntactic category that occur in your text. Good categories include single-word adjectives, single-word adverbs or adverb phrases. Make one copy of the doctored text for each student. Alternatively, write the doctored text up on the board. Without single-word adverbs, 'I remember, I remember' looks like this:

I remember, I remember
The house where I was born,
The little window where the sun
Came peeping in at morn;
He . . . came a wink too . . . ,
Nor brought too long a day;
But . . . , I . . . wish the night
Had borne my breath . . . !

I remember, I remember
The roses, red and white,
The violets, and the lily-cups,
Those flowers made of light!
The lilacs where the robin built,
And where my brother set
The laburnum on his birthday,—
The tree is living . . . !

I remember, I remember
Where I was used to swing,
And thought the air must rush as fresh
To swallows on the wing;
My spirit flew in feathers . . . ,
That is so heavy . . . ,
And summer pools could . . . cool
The fever on my brow!

I remember, I remember
The fir trees dark and high;
I used to think their slender tops
Were close against the sky:
It was a childish ignorance,
But . . . 'tis little joy
To know I'm farther off from heav'n
Than when I was a boy.

## Procedure

1 Divide the class into groups of four to six and tell the students which category of word has been omitted. Each group tries to supply suitable items.
2 When a group finishes, it divides and combines with half the members of another group to compare results. Alternatively, each group can write their results on the board and the whole class can decide which suggestions are most acceptable.

## 2.12

**TIME**
45 minutes

**LEVEL**
Intermediate +

**MATERIALS**
A copy of the text
that can be
written on

**SUGGESTED
TEXTS**
Any short poem

# SUBSTITUTING

The aim of this exercise is to raise the students' awareness of how words have a poetic function by exploring the possibilities of replacing words.

## Procedure

1 Working individually, each student replaces four words in the original text with their own words. They may choose which words in the text to replace, but they must replace:
   - one single-syllable word
   - one two-syllable word
   - one three-syllable word
   - one word that rhymes

When they have done this, they write their decisions down on a small piece of paper in the following format (the examples here are from 'I remember, I remember'):

Single-syllable word: line 19, air ➤ sky
(indicating that *air* has been replaced by *sky*)
Two-syllable word: line 7, often ➤ sometimes
Three-syllable word: line 29, ignorance ➤ happiness
Rhyming word: line 4, morn ➤ dawn

The examples of words chosen and the substitutes are ours, of course.

2 When the first few students have done this, ask them to leave the papers displaying their suggested substitutions on view on their desks and to circulate, looking at other people's substitutions and incorporating any they really like into the text itself. This requires considerable concentration.

3 Ask anyone who has made several alterations to their text to read it aloud.

**NOTE**
If you were to substitute an item in a non-literary text, it would need to satisfy only semantic criteria. In a literary text it also needs to satisfy stylistic criteria. This makes this exercise especially thought-provoking.

# CONTRASTING

The aim of this exercise is to make the students think about the meaning of the poem through exploring what effect saying the opposite would have.

## Procedure

This exercise works best if you provide photocopies of the text. Working individually, the students circle as many words in the text as they can provide opposites for and write the opposites on the photocopy. Encourage the students to be brave in their choice of opposites (see Notes below). The word in the text and its opposite should be circled and linked like this:

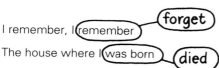

Because of the surprising diversity of responses, it is a good idea to display the results on the wall and allow reading time.

### NOTES

1 Opposites, or antonyms, may be the opposite of any particular feature of a word's meaning. The opposites of *man*, for example, include *woman*, *boy*, *animal*, and *god*.

2 One way of defining a meaning is to consider how it relates to another meaning. If you try and define the meanings of words in a text by considering their opposites, it often gives a much clearer picture of the world constructed by the text.

## 2.13

**TIME**
25–30 minutes

**LEVEL**
Higher
elementary +

**MATERIALS**
A class set of
copies of the text
that can be
written on

**SUGGESTED
TEXTS**
Any short poem

## 2.14

**TIME**
10 minutes per
line + 10 minutes
discussion time

**LEVEL**
Higher
elementary –
Intermediate

**MATERIALS**
A class set of
specially-typed
handouts of a
poem

**SUGGESTED
TEXTS**
Any short poem
with 4–8 verses

# COMPLETING

The aim of this exercise is to concentrate the students' minds on what
the writer would say at a decisive moment in the text.

## Preparation

Photocopy or write up on the board the complete text of the poem but
with each word in the last line of each verse represented only by its first
letter:

I remember, I remember
The house where I was born,
The little window where the sun
Came peeping in at morn;
He never came a wink too soon,
Nor brought too long a day;
But now, I often wish the night
H  b   m   b   a

I remember, I remember
The roses, red and white,
The violets, and the lily-cups,
Those flowers made of light!
The lilacs where the robin built,
And where my brother set
The laburnum on his birthday, —
T  t  i  l  y

I remember, I remember
Where I was used to swing,
And thought the air must rush as fresh
To swallows on the wing;
My spirit flew in feathers then,
That is so heavy now,
And summer pools could hardly cool
T  f  o  m  b

I remember, I remember
The fir trees dark and high;
I used to think their slender tops
Were close against the sky:
It was a childish ignorance,
But now 'tis little joy
To know I'm farther off from heav'n
T  w  l  w  a  b

## Procedure

1 Working individually or in pairs, tell the students to complete the last line of each verse with words beginning with the letters given in the text.
2 When everyone has finished, in classes of fewer than twenty, read the suggested lines round the class. With larger classes, it is better to ask the students to work in groups of five or six to compare their work.

## EVALUATING

In this exercise, the students make judgments about the extent to which every word in the text contributes to a thematic whole. The aim of the exercise is to raise awareness of the extent to which a text coheres semantically and the way in which the secondary as well as the primary meanings of words are important.

## Procedure

1 The students may work individually or in pairs. Ask each individual/pair to pick a general word under which some of the text's vocabulary could be listed. Sometimes it helps if you suggest three or four possible category words; for 'I remember, I remember', *nature, time* and *plants* would be suitable.
2 Each learner/pair then lists all the vocabulary that falls within the general words chosen. Allow the students to use dictionaries if they want to.
3 Next, ask each learner/pair to consider every word/phrase in the text that they have not listed, i.e. the remaining text. This time, they should try in some way to *associate* every word/phrase with the chosen general word. For example, if my chosen general word was *nature*, 'The little window' might be listed this time because when I was a child my bedroom window looked out over fields. Ask the students to list these words/phrases in a second column. When this has been done, there will not be much of the poem that is not listed.

### VARIATIONS
1 Ask the students to work through a number of texts, deciding on a general word for each that would include several vocabulary items.
2 Ask the students to decide on a short phrase for each text rather than a general word.

### NOTE
Words have two kinds of meaning: a literal meaning ('denotation') and a secondary meaning ('connotation'). Very often the connotation is more important in everyday language use than the denotation. For example, if you knew only the literal meaning of 'happy hour', you would not know its more important connotation – that it is the time

### 2.15

**TIME**
30–40 minutes

**LEVEL**
Beginner/
Elementary+

when you can get two drinks in a bar for the price of one. In the early stages of language learning we often think too much of literal, dictionary meanings and too little of real world meanings. In this exercise, it is not only denotation but more especially connotation that is important.

## 2.16

**TIME**
10–20 minutes

**LEVEL**
Beginner +

**SUGGESTED TEXTS**
Very short poems or single verses

# REDUCING

The aim of this exercise is to stimulate awareness of the time it takes to say a word by representing progressively larger parts of the text with silence, as in 'John Brown's Body'. This is important in a stress-timed language like English where the length of time is determined by whether the word is part or all of a stress unit.

## Procedure

Read the text aloud chorally. With each reading drop one more word from the end of each line and remain silent for as long as it would take to say the word. So the second time 'I remember, I remember' is read aloud it will sound like this:

I remember, I_____
The house where I was_____
The little window where the_____
Came peeping in at _____
He never came a wink too _____
Nor brought too long a _____
But now I often wish the _____
Had borne my breath _____

and the third time like this:

I remember, _____
The house where I _____
The little window where _____
Came peeping in _____
He never came a wink _____
Nor brought too long _____
But now I often wish _____
Had borne my _____

The fact that the lines are of unequal lengths adds greatly to the interest.

**TIPS**
- If you allow the students to put a line through the words that they are leaving off at each reading, they do not get confused when the lines become very short.
- Practice makes perfect, so do not be afraid of reading the text a few times until the students really concentrate and get it right.

**SUGGESTED TEXTS**

Here are three further poems on the theme of memory which you may
like to work with:

Into my heart an air that kills
From yon far country blows;
What are those blue remembered hills,
What spires, what farms are those?

That is the land of lost content,
I see it shining plain,
The happy highways where I went
And cannot come again

A E Housman, (from *A Shropshire Lad*)

## REMEMBER

Remember me when I am gone away,
Gone far away into the silent land;
When you no more can hold me by the hand,
Nor I half turn to go yet turning stay.
Remember me when no more day by day
You tell me of our future that you planned.
Only remember me; you understand
It will be late to counsel then or pray.
Yet if you should forget me for a while
And afterwards remember, do not grieve;
For if the darkness and corruption leave
A vestige of the thoughts that once I had,
Better by far you should forget and smile
Than that you should remember and be sad.

Christina Rossetti

## SUDDEN LIGHT

I have been here before,
But when or how I cannot tell.
I know the grass beyond the door,
The sweet keen smell
The sighing sound, the lights around the shore.

You have been mine before —
How long ago I may not know;
But just when at that swallow's soar
Your neck turned so,
Some veil did fall — I knew it all of yore.

Then, now, — perchance again! . . .
O round mine eyes your tresses shake!
Shall we not lie as we have lain
Thus for Love's sake,
And sleep, and wake, yet never break the chain!

Dante Gabriel Rossetti

# CHAPTER 3

# *Pre-reading*

Although pre-reading may not be necessary for every text based activity, there are several reasons why it is important:

1 If the students prepare to meet the text carefully, they feel they already know what to expect when the 'real reading' begins. This makes learning easier and more natural.

2 Pre-reading allows the students to meet the text on more equal terms, often by contributing their own experiences, ideas and guesses to a text before actually reading it.

3 Pre-reading is a 'learning to learn' skill. It's about *how* to read or meet texts and therefore promotes the learners' awareness of their responsibility for their own learning.

4 It is easy to make pre-reading a collaborative activity in which learners pool or exchange their ideas about the text they are to read.

5 Pre-reading, and especially the prediction element, is inherently interesting and creates a sense of expectation and excitement about the text.

6 Pre-reading creates a situation in which students read texts for a meaning which is matched against expectation. It therefore turns the 'real reading' that follows into a task reading exercise in which the text is matched against what it is expected to contain.

7 Pre-reading is one area where you can be eclectic in drawing on techniques without compromising your overriding methodology. You can use Suggestopedia 'concert' techniques, for example, or guided fantasy as pre-reading techniques without needing to take on other aspects of the methodologies from which they are drawn.

8 Many of us have a natural resistance to what is new or unknown. Pre-reading helps to reduce the extent to which the new or unknown element in literature challenges our sense of order and makes us react defensively.

9 There is a crude variety of pre-teaching (as in demonstrating unfamiliar vocabulary by showing pictures of the objects referred to, to take one example); more thoughtful pre-teaching gives the students a deeper level of involvement in language by enabling them to compare their own and the text's constructions of reality.

10 Pre-reading allows for concentration on a single level, such as lexis or discourse structure, and can therefore serve an important function in providing an intensive learning experience at a single level.

One way of grouping the exercises in this chapter is according to whether they *work from a text* which is provided at the pre-reading stage but which has still to be read intensively or whether they are *text-free prediction* exercises. There are five *working from a text* exercises (3.1 *Poem and collage,* 3.2 *Taking sides,* 3.3 *Supplying the answers,* 3.4 *Profiling the writer,* 3.7 *Restoring the original*) and three *text-free prediction* exercises (3.5 *Poems and their word sets,* 3.6 *The unexpected,* 3.8 *Understanding unusual texts*).

As you work through these exercises, you will notice that we have exemplified pre-reading techniques with quite hard texts; this is because pre-reading is more often needed with difficult texts than easy ones.

Finally, when you have become familiar with these exercises, you might try dividing them up according to the level each one focuses on. Which ones focus on lexis? Which on semantic fields, prosody or discourse structures? And which do not seem to focus on any particular level?

# POEM AND COLLAGE

This exercise allows students to read a poem impressionistically and interpret it in their own way before anyone tries to impose a received viewpoint on them. Its aim is therefore to give the students an intuitive feel for the poem before the serious reading and discussion begin.

## Procedure

1 Distribute a sheet of A3, a colour magazine and a copy of the poem to each student. Allow the students twenty-five minutes to make a collage using any pictures (and if they wish, words) from the colour magazine that they feel match the mood of the poem. The text should also appear somewhere in each collage.
2 As the students finish, they can display their work on the wall.

**VARIATION**
This exercise can also work as a collective activity for a group of three to six students if you give them Blu-tack and board to work on instead of paper and glue. If one group makes a collage this way while other groups are doing other things, then subsequently groups can explain to each other what they did and why.

**NOTE**
Poems that work well for this exercise are those that evoke colour or landscape, such as Thomas Hardy's 'Neutral Tones', Alice Meynell's 'Parted', or Wallace Stevens's 'Domination of Black'.

## 3.1

**TIME**
25–30 minutes

**LEVEL**
Beginner +

**MATERIALS**
A3 sheets of paper, scissors, glue, colour magazines, a class set of handouts of copies of a poem

**SUGGESTED TEXTS**
Short, fairly complex poems

## NEUTRAL TONES

We stood by a pond that winter day,
And the sun was white, as though chidden of God,
And a few leaves lay on the starving sod;
    — They had fallen from an ash, and were gray.

Your eyes on me were as eyes that rove
Over tedious riddles of years ago;
And some words played between us to and fro
    On which lost the more by our love.

The smile on your mouth was the deadest thing
Alive enough to have strength to die;
And a grin of bitterness swept thereby
    Like an ominous bird a-wing....

Since then, keen lessons that love deceives,
And wrings with wrong, have shaped to me
Your face, and the God-curst sun, and a tree,
    And a pond edged with grayish leaves.

Thomas Hardy


## PARTED

Farewell to one now silenced quite,
Sent out of hearing, out of sight, –
    My friend of friends, whom I shall miss.
    He is not banished, though, for this, –
Nor he, nor sadness, nor delight.

Though I shall walk with him no more,
A low voice sounds upon the shore.
    He must not watch my resting-place
    But who shall drive a mournful face
From the sad winds about my door?

I shall not hear his voice complain
But who shall stop the patient rain?
    His tears must not disturb my heart,
    But who shall change the years, and part
The world from every thought of pain?

Although my life is left so dim,
The morning crowns the mountain-rim;
    Joy is not gone from summer skies,
    Nor innocence from children's eyes,
And all these things are part of him.

He is not banished, for the showers
Yet wake this green warm earth of ours.
  How can the summer but be sweet?
  I shall not have him at my feet,
And yet my feet are on the flowers.

Alice Meynell

# TAKING SIDES

In this exercise, the students empathise with each of two characters in a situation in a novel or play before they read the complete text. The aim of the exercise is to make the text easier to understand, to discourage a one-sided response and to encourage careful, considered reading.

## Preparation

1 Choose an emotional exchange between two characters from the short story, (chapter of a) novel or play the class is reading. Select six to eight contributions to this exchange made by one of the two characters.
2 Copy each speech on to the top of a separate sheet of paper and make enough photocopies of each sheet for there to be one for each student. It may sometimes be a good idea to simplify the text slightly or, by altering place names etc., to make it relevant to the local situation.

## Procedure

1 Ask the students to sit in a circle and distribute the sheets so that each student gets a different speech from their neighbour.
2 Ask each student to read their speech silently and then pass it to the person sitting on their left, who should write a considered reply and then return the sheet. Each student is thus engaged in a 'dialogue in writing' with each of their neighbours.
3 Allow these dialogues-in-writing to continue until either there is no more room on the sheets or the pairs start to come to a natural conclusion.
4 Ask the students either to act the dialogues out or read them aloud.

### EXAMPLE
For truly advanced students, the episode in Jane Austen's *Pride and Prejudice* where Mr Collins proposes unsuccessfully to Elizabeth works well. Each paper would start with one of the following declarations:

---

**3.2**

**TIME**
30–45 minutes depending on the difficulty or complexity of the text

**LEVEL**
Intermediate +

**MATERIALS**
Copies of single speeches (see Preparation)

**SUGGESTED TEXTS**
Drama, short stories, chapters of novels

'...allow me to assure you that I have your respected mother's permission for this address. You can hardly doubt the purport of my discourse, however your natural delicacy may lead you to dissemble; my attentions have been too marked to be mistaken. Almost as soon as I entered the house I singled you out as the companion of my future life.'

'...before I am run away with by my feelings on this subject, perhaps it will be advisable for me to state my reasons for marrying — and moreover for coming into Hertfordshire with the design of selecting a wife, as I certainly did.'

'...it remains to be told why my views were directed to Longbourn instead of my own neighbourhood, where I assure you there are many amiable young women. But the fact is, that being, as I am, to inherit this estate after the death of your honoured father, (who, however, may live many years longer,) I could not satisfy myself without resolving to chuse a wife from among his daughters, that the loss to them might be as little as possible, when the melancholy event takes place — which, however, as I have already said, may not be for several years. This has been my motive, my fair cousin, and I flatter myself it will not sink me in your esteem.'

'And now nothing remains for me but to assure you in the most animated language of the violence of my affection. To fortune I am perfectly indifferent, and shall make no demand of that nature on your father, since I am well aware that it could not be complied with; and that one thousand pounds in the 4 per cents which will not be yours till after your mother's decease, is all that you may ever be entitled to. On that head, therefore, I shall be uniformly silent; and you may assure yourself that no ungenerous reproach shall ever pass my lips when we are married.'

'My reasons for marrying are, first, that I think it a right thing for every clergyman in easy circumstances (like myself) to set the example of matrimony in his parish. Secondly, that I am convinced it will add very greatly to my happiness; and thirdly — which perhaps I ought to have mentioned earlier, that it is the particular advice and recommendation of the very noble lady whom I have the honour of calling patroness.'

'I am not now to learn that it is usual with young ladies to reject the addresses of the man whom they secretly mean to accept, when he first applies for their favour; and that sometimes the refusal is repeated a second or even a third time. I am therefore by no means discouraged and shall hope to lead you to the altar ere long.'

'When I do myself the honour of speaking to you next on this subject I shall hope to receive a more favourable answer than you have now given me; though I am far from accusing you of cruelty at present, because I know it to be the established custom of your sex to reject a man on the first application, and perhaps you have even now said as much to encourage my suit as would be consistent with the true delicacy of the female character.'

'You must give me leave to flatter myself, my dear cousin, that your refusal of my addresses is merely words of course. My reasons for believing it are briefly these: it does not appear to me that my hand is unworthy your acceptance, or that the establishment I can offer would be any other than highly desirable. My situation in life, my connections with the family of De Bourgh, and my relationship to your own, are circumstances highly in my favour; and you should take it into farther consideration that in spite of your manifold attractions, it is by no means certain that another offer of marriage may ever be made you. Your portion is unhappily so small that it will in all likelihood undo the effects of your loveliness and amiable qualifications. As I must therefore conclude that you are not serious in your rejection of me, I shall chuse to attribute it to your wish of increasing my love by suspense, according to the usual practice of elegant females.'

We have found that students frequently ask if they are to write in character or as themselves. We have found it best not to prescribe a strategy.

ACKNOWLEDGEMENT
We learnt this idea from Gerry Kenny, who used it with the text of a pop song at a Pilgrims Staff Development seminar.

# SUPPLYING THE ANSWERS

Prediction exercises are a well-known way of preparing the reader or listener for the text to be read or heard. Texts that contain questions make particularly good prediction exercises because they invite answers from the reader. We illustrate the technique with Barry Cole's poem 'Reported Missing'.

## 3.3

**TIME**
30–40 minutes

**LEVEL**
Intermediate +

**MATERIALS**
A class set of a specially prepared handout

**SUGGESTED TEXTS**
Poems with question and answer structures

REPORTED MISSING

Can you give me a precise description?
Said the policeman. Her lips, I told him,
Were soft. Could you give me, he said, pencil
Raised, a metaphor? Soft as an open mouth,
I said. Were there any noticeable
Peculiarities? he asked. Her hair hung
Heavily, I said. Any particular
Colour? he said. I told him I could recall
Little but its distinctive scent. What do
You mean, he asked, by distinctive? It had
The smell of woman's hair, I said. Where
Were you? he asked. Closer than I am to
Anyone at present, I said, level
With her mouth, level with her eyes. Her eyes?
He said, what about her eyes? There were two,
I said, both black. It has been established,

He said, that eyes cannot, outside common
Usage, be black; are you implying that
Violence was used? Only the gentle
Hammer blow of her kisses, the scent
Of her breath, the ... Quite, said the policeman,
Standing, but I regret that we know of
No one answering to that description.

Barry Cole

## Preparation

Prepare your text by deleting the answers to all the questions it contains. Make a copy of the prepared text for each student. 'Reported Missing' would therefore look like this:

Can you give me a precise description? said the policeman.

Could you give me, he said, pencil raised, a metaphor?

Were there any noticeable peculiarities? he asked.

Any particular colour? he said.

What do you mean, he asked, by distinctive?

Where were you? he asked.

Her eyes? he said, what about her eyes?

It has been established, he said, that eyes cannot, outside common usage, be black; are you implying that violence was used?

Quite, said the policeman, standing, but I regret that we know of no one answering to that description.

## Procedure

1 Group the students in fours and give them the prepared gapped text. Allow them twenty minutes to complete it.
2 Allow the groups a few more minutes to get ready to read the text aloud. They should decide how to divide up the reading task and then practise reading so that their performance will be fluent.
3 The groups read out their texts in turn.

### VARIATION
Distribute the prepared gapped text and allow students ten minutes to work individually on completing it. Then read the text aloud pausing at the gaps for students to supply their suggestions.

### NOTE
This sort of exercise can also be used after structures such as *like...*, *(s)he seemed to be...*, and *when...* . Prepare the poem by deleting the material following these words and phrases.

# PROFILING THE WRITER

3.4

**TIME**
40 minutes

**LEVEL**
Intermediate +

**MATERIALS**
A handout containing a copy of the opening of a novel, story, poem or play (optional)

**SUGGESTED TEXTS**
Any poem, story, play or novel written in the first person

This is an exercise that prepares the students for reading a text written in the first person. The aim of the exercise is to help the students get inside the person they suppose the 'I' character to be. They may do this successfully or entirely unsuccessfully but in either case their interest will be heightened and as they read the text they will be encouraged to make a comparison with the profile they had imagined.

## Procedure

1 Either distribute copies of the opening lines of the autobiographical text you want to work with or write it up on the board. Instruct each student to rewrite it in the third person using the pronouns and possessives (masculine or feminine) that seem appropriate. This helps to give a clearer and more objective picture of the character.
2 Ask each student to draw the person. Do not accept any protests about inability to draw.
3 Ask each student to write a paragraph beginning with the words, '(S)he is going to...'. This paragraph should describe what the student thinks the character is going to do in the poem, story, novel or play.
4 Group the students in threes and ask them to compare their drawing and writing.
5 If the text is a poem, you can now read it. If it is a novel, display the drawing and writing on the wall and at the end of each chapter give the students the opportunity to remove theirs and make any necessary alterations.

### SUGGESTED TEXTS

These are examples only; any first-person text you are reading is suitable.

- I wandered lonely as a cloud
  That floats on high o'er dales and hills,
  When all at once I saw a crowd,
  A host, of golden daffodils;
  William Wordsworth, 'Daffodils'

- That's my last Duchess painted on the wall
  Looking as if she were alive. I call
  That piece a wonder, now;
  Robert Browning, 'My Last Duchess'

- Softly, in the dusk, a woman is singing to me
  Taking me back down the vista of years till I see
  A child
  D H Lawrence, 'The Piano'

- I have a great deal of difficulty in beginning to write my
  portion of these pages, for I know I am not clever. I always knew that.
  Charles Dickens, *Bleak House*

- As I walked through the wilderness of this world, I lighted on a certain place where was a den, and I laid me down in that place to sleep, and as I slept I dreamed a dream.

  John Bunyan, *The Pilgrim's Progress*

- My true name is so well known in the records, or registers, at Newgate and in the Old Bailey, and there are some things of such consequence still depending there relating to my particular conduct, that it is not to be expected that I should set my name or the account of my family to this work.

  Daniel Defoe, *Moll Flanders*

## 3.5

**TIME**
30 minutes

**LEVEL**
Intermediate +

**SUGGESTED TEXTS**
Two texts with overlapping but distinct contents

# POEMS AND THEIR WORD SETS

The aim of this exercise is to create expectations about the lexical and thematic content of the texts that are to be read.

## Preparation

Choose two texts the contents of which differ but also overlap. Select an equal number of vocabulary items from each.

## Procedure

1 Write the vocabulary items you have selected on the board in alphabetical order. The students should work in small groups. Tell them that the vocabulary items come from two different poems and that they should decide which items belong in which poem. Allow about fifteen minutes for this. If any groups finish earlier, ask one group to compare their results with another.

2 You now read the poems aloud while the students check their predictions. Discuss unexpected results.

### EXAMPLE
For higher intermediate and advanced students, a possible pair of texts is Oscar Wilde's 'Symphony in Yellow' and the first verse of Matthew Arnold's 'Dover Beach'.

## DOVER BEACH

The sea is calm to-night.
The tide is full, the moon lies fair
Upon the straits; — on the French coast the light
Gleams and is gone; the cliffs of England stand,
Glimmering and vast, out in the tranquil bay.
Come to the window, sweet is the night-air!
Only, from the long line of spray
Where the sea meets the moon-blanch'd land,
Listen! you hear the grating roar
Of pebbles which the waves draw back, and fling,
At their return, up the high strand,
Begin, and cease, and then again begin,
With tremulous cadence slow, and bring
The eternal note of sadness in.

Matthew Arnold

## SYMPHONY IN YELLOW

An omnibus across the bridge
   Crawls like a yellow butterfly,
   And, here and there, a passer-by
Shows like a little restless midge.

Big barges full of yellow hay
   Are moved against the shadowy wharf,
   And, like a yellow silken scarf,
The thick fog hangs along the quay.

The yellow leaves begin to fade
   And flutter from the Temple elms,
   And at my feet the pale green Thames
Lies like a rod of rippled jade.

Oscar Wilde

## Suggested vocabulary items:

| barges | cliffs | moon | sadness | waves |
|--------|--------|------|---------|-------|
| bay | fog | passer-by | spray | wharf |
| bridge | hay | pebbles | strand | window |
| butterfly | leaves | quay | tide | yellow |

## VARIATIONS

1 Choose an abstract word from each poem and tell the students at Step 1 that each list should group around this abstract word. For example, *sadness* for 'Dover Beach' and *yellow* for 'Symphony in Yellow'.

2 Before you read the text aloud, ask each group to suggest three or four further words they expect to hear in it.

## 3.6

**TIME**
25 minutes

**LEVEL**
Elementary +

**MATERIALS**
Enough photo-copies of two short poems for half the class to get one, and half the class to get the other

# THE UNEXPECTED

The aim of the exercise is to give each student a detailed expectation as to what will be in a text so that this can be checked against the text itself and any discrepancies discussed. The exercise also has a secondary aim: to make the students aware of the benefit of a pre-reading exercise since they read two texts in the exercise, one with the benefit of pre-reading and one without.

## Preparation

Choose two short poems. Make sure there are enough copies of each for one to be shared between every two students.

## Procedure

1 Pair the students. Distribute one text to one student, the other to their partner. Each student reads only the text given to them. Allow up to ten minutes for the texts to be read carefully three or four times.
2 Ask the students to put their texts aside and tell their partners what their poem was about, using as many of the original words as they recall.
3 The students exchange texts and each reads the poem their partner told them about.
4 Finally, the students explain to their partners what they found in the text that they were not expecting to find.

**SUGGESTED TEXTS**
With higher intermediate and advanced students, you might like to work with Elizabeth Jennings' 'The Unknown Child' and Sylvia Plath's 'Child'.

**NOTE**
We have called this a text-free prediction exercise because, although each student reads a text and works from it, the real benefit is derived by their partner who hears about the text and develops expectations before reading it.

# RESTORING THE ORIGINAL

The aim of this exercise is to give the students an idea of what is in the text they are going to read by having them think deeply about each small part of it first.

## Preparation

Divide the text you are going to read into as many small units (around two lines for poems and one sentence for prose) as there are students in the class. Copy each of these on to a separate piece of paper and number them consecutively. If the number of students who turn up in class does not match the number of units of text exactly, you can pair students or give one student two consecutive units. Whatever you do, you must not end up with students without text or text without students.

## Procedure

1 Ask the students to sit in a circle. Ask everyone to take a sheet of paper and write in the margin the numbers from 1 to whatever the number of units there are (this is Sheet 1).
2 Distribute the pieces of poem (Sheet 2) so that they are spread consecutively around the circle. Tell each student to substitute a word of their own choice for one word in the original in such a way as to retain the sense. They then copy the altered version along with the number of the unit on to another sheet of paper (Sheet 3).
3 Each Sheet 3 (but not the original text on Sheet 2) is then repeatedly passed on round the circle. Each time a student gets a new piece of poem, they:
   i try to reverse the original Step 2 change by changing one word and writing their suggested version on Sheet 3;
   ii copy their suggested version down in the right place on their own numbered sheet (Sheet 1).
4 When each piece of poem has been all round the class, you should read the original text aloud.

**EXAMPLE**
Over the page is an example of how a text suitable for Higher intermediate and Advanced students might be divided up into fragments (the slashes '/' indicate the divisions).

**TIME**
40–60 minutes

**LEVEL**
Intermediate +

**MATERIALS**
Enough pieces of poem for each student to get one (see Preparation)

**SUGGESTED TEXTS**
Any poem with about twice as many lines as there are students in the class, or any piece of prose with as many sentences as there are students

## A PRAYER FOR MY DAUGHTER

Once more the storm is howling, and half hid
Under this cradle-hood and coverlid
My child sleeps on./ There is no obstacle
But Gregory's wood and one bare hill
Whereby the haystack and roof-levelling wind,
Bred on the Atlantic, can be stayed;/
And for an hour I have walked and prayed
Because of the great gloom that is in my mind./

I have walked and prayed for this young child an hour
And heard the sea-wind scream upon the tower,
And under the arches of the bridge, and scream
In the elms above the flooded stream;/
Imagining in excited reverie
That the future years had come,
Dancing to a frenzied drum,
Out of the murderous innocence of the sea./

May she be granted beauty and yet not
Beauty to make a stranger's eye distraught,
Or hers before a looking-glass,/ for such,
Being made beautiful overmuch,
Consider beauty a sufficient end,/
Lose natural kindness and maybe
The heart-revealing intimacy
That chooses right, and never find a friend./

Helen being chosen found life flat and dull
And later had much trouble from a fool,/
While that great Queen, that rose out of the spray,
Being fatherless could have her way
Yet chose a bandy-leggèd smith for man./
It's certain that fine women eat
A crazy salad with their meat
Whereby the Horn of Plenty is undone./

In courtesy I'd have her chiefly learned;/
Hearts are not had as a gift but hearts are earned
By those that are not entirely beautiful;/
Yet many, that have played the fool
For beauty's very self, has charm made wise,/
And many a poor man that has roved,
Loved and thought himself beloved,
From a glad kindness cannot take his eyes./

May she become a flourishing hidden tree
That all her thoughts may like the linnet be,/
And have no business but dispensing round
Their magnanimities of sound,/
Nor but in merriment begin a chase,/
Nor but in merriment a quarrel./
O may she live like some green laurel
Rooted in one dear perpetual place./

My mind, because the minds that I have loved,
The sort of beauty that I have approved,
Prosper but little, has dried up of late,/
Yet knows that to be choked with hate
May well be of all evil chances chief./
If there's no hatred in a mind
Assault and battery of the wind
Can never tear the linnet from the leaf./

An intellectual hatred is the worst,
So let her think opinions are accursed./
Have I not seen the loveliest woman born
Out of the mouth of Plenty's horn,/
Because of her opinionated mind
Barter that horn and every good
By quiet natures understood
For an old bellows full of angry wind?/

Considering that, all hatred driven hence,
The soul recovers radical innocence
And learns at last that it is self-delighting,/
Self-appeasing, self-affrighting,
And that its own sweet will is Heaven's will;/
She can, though every face should scowl
And every windy quarter howl
Or every bellows burst, be happy still./

And may her bridegroom bring her to a house
Where all's accustomed, ceremonious;/
For arrogance and hatred are the wares
Peddled in the thoroughfares./
How but in custom and in ceremony
Are innocence and beauty born?/
Ceremony's a name for the rich horn,
And custom for the spreading laurel tree./

W B Yeats

**VARIATIONS**
1 This exercise can be simplified by cutting out Step 1. In other words, do not ask the students to make Sheet 1. To begin with, each student is given a piece of poem and substitutes one of the original words with a word of their own choice. Each student copies their altered version on to a sheet of paper, and these sheets are then passed round so that each student can change just one word when each sheet reaches them. This makes the instruction-giving much simpler, but the results, although still fascinating, are less interesting than when each student constructs a version of the whole text.
2 An even simpler variation is to take one phrase or line from a poem and explore all the possible substitutions. For example, 'through the door we never opened': *through* ➤ *past, beside; door* ➤ *gate; never* ➤ *always, nearly;* etc.

**3.8**

**TIME**
30–40 minutes

**LEVEL**
Higher
intermediate +

**MATERIALS**
Prepared
questions (on the
board or on a
handout)

**SUGGESTED
TEXTS**
Any text which
conveys a
message in a
bizarre or
paradoxical way

# UNDERSTANDING UNUSUAL TEXTS

The aim of this exercise is to prepare the imagination for a highly unusual text. The more complex or unusual the text, the more appropriate it is. We illustrate this exercise with Craig Raine's 'A Martian Sends a Postcard Home'.

## Preparation

If you are not using the example text, write out a set of (preferably multiple-choice) questions for your chosen text.

## Procedure

1 Ask the students to work in groups of four to six. Either distribute a set of questions to each group or write them up on the board and tell the students they have twenty-five minutes to decide on the likeliest answers.
2 At the end of the twenty-five minutes, read the poem aloud very slowly indeed. You can distribute the text before or after your reading. With a text like 'A Martian Sends a Postcard Home' it is probably better to distribute the text before you read because the verse structure matches the questions so closely.

## QUESTIONS

1 Is a Caxton   a book?
             a helicopter?
             a violin?

2 Is night   mist
     when the sky is tired of flight?
     sleep

3 Is rain   night
    when the earth is television?
    winter

4 Is a cupboard   a car
    a room with the lock inside?
    love

5 Is a shirt   a bomb
    tied to the wrist?
    time

6 Is the ghost   the baby?
    granny?
    your soul?

7 Is a haunted apparatus   a cat?
    a person?
    a telephone?

8 What happens in the punishment room?

9 What are you doing when you read about yourself in colour with your eyelids shut?

© Longman Group UK Ltd 1993

## A MARTIAN SENDS A POSTCARD HOME

Caxtons are mechanical birds with many wings
and some are treasured for their markings.

They cause the eyes to melt
or the body to shriek without pain.

I have never seen one fly, but
sometimes they perch on the hand.

Mist is when the sky is tired of flight
and rests its soft machine on the ground:

then the world is dim and bookish
like engravings under tissue paper.

Rain is when the earth is television.
It has the property of making colours darker.

Model T is a room with the lock inside —
a key is turned to free the world

for movement, so quick there is a film
to watch for anything missed.

But time is tied to the wrist
Or kept in a box, ticking with impatience.

In homes, a haunted apparatus sleeps,
that snores when you pick it up.

If the ghost cries, they carry it
to their lips and soothe it to sleep

with sounds. And yet, they wake it up
deliberately, by tickling with a finger.

Only the young are allowed to suffer
openly. Adults go to a punishment room

with water but nothing to eat.
They lock the door and suffer the noises

alone. No one is exempt
and everyone's pain has a different smell.

At night, when all the colours die,
they hide in pairs

and read about themselves —
in colour, with their eyelids shut.

Craig Raine

**VARIATION**

For elementary and intermediate students, use the same technique, but instead of working with a bizarre or paradoxical text as here, choose a more straightforward text and devise questions on vocabulary. For example, working with William Wordsworth's 'Daffodils':

being surprised?
Is wandering something you do in the bath?
walking slowly?

# CHAPTER 4

# *Reading*

If an educated adult has a reading problem in the mother tongue, it will almost always result from unfamiliar subject matter. But if an early-stage second language learner has a reading problem, it is very likely to be a technical one. Perhaps the student is unfamiliar with the grapheme–phoneme relationships, or perhaps the constituent structure of the text is difficult to process. For this reason, practising oral reading, or reading out loud, is very important. In addition, the true nature of a literary text can only be revealed in performance because its prosody is inherently original, difficult, and needs to be worked on. Finally, group reading also helps to create a collaborative classroom and work ethic.

With all these thoughts in mind, therefore, and because there are so many oral reading techniques, we have decided that it is more useful and more economical to list these techniques than to produce dozens of reading-for-performance exercises.

## Reading as performance: general techniques

1  Choral work: where a text or part of a text is spoken aloud simultaneously by more than one reader.
2  Reading in canon: where one group of readers starts reading the text that another group has already begun to read.
3  Ways of dividing readers into groups for choral work: A good strategy is to suggest or agree a criterion with the class and then each student decides if they fall into it. Criteria include:
   - *physical attributes* (eye/hair/skin colour, features of dress, spectacle/non-spectacle wearers),
   - *biographical facts* (dates of birth, provenance, family status),
   - *affective factors* (mood – happy/sad; personality type – optimistic/pessimistic; feelings/experiences on the day),
   - *feelings about/reactions to the text* (positive/negative, sympathetic/unsympathetic).
4  Ways of dividing the text between several groups of readers:
   - Have repeated lines or refrains read collectively.
   - Divide the text according to first words of lines (e.g. one speaker or group reads lines beginning with 'And...', etc.).
   - Divide it according to the stanza structure, with some stanzas read by groups and some in canon.
   - Decide which parts of a text are 'crescendo' and which are 'diminuendo' and allocate readers accordingly.

- Take the text away word by word (as with 'John Brown's Body' on page 48).
- Best of all, allow groups of students / the whole class to decide which parts of the text will be read by which groups.

**5** You can use the cassette recorder:
- to combine a recorded reading of part of the text (by yourself, or a well-known actor, or a member of the class) with individual or group contributions from the class.
- to establish a first choral or individual reading which is then to be bettered, rearranged or given a radically different rendering.
- when you divide the class into two groups and have each group make a recording for the other group.

**6** You can use your own voice:
- for the students to pick out words or phrases from a text (see Exercise 4.10 *Key words*).
- as a lead voice to guide the reading.
- for the students to join in with at the moments they choose, perhaps according to some prearranged criterion.
- for students to chime in with on particular cues, which might be lexical or positional.
- to set a tempo for the students to follow.

**7** Useful non-linguistic techniques include:
- *Clapping:* clap the rhythm; respond to particular words/lines with applause; interpose clapping and text; clap hands/thighs/another's shoulder blades. Alternatives to clapping include drumming fingers on desks, tapping feet on floor, rubbing hands together.
- *Music:* use as an accompaniment; use to give a text rhythm (e.g. making a jazz chant or rap out of it); use only the words of a song at first and later bring in the music.
- *Pictures:* use pictures as prompts or accompaniment to illustrate themes, colours, actions, people, moods. The pictures can be held up at appropriate moments or displayed around the classroom and addressed.
- *Silence:* decide which parts of a text to respond to with silence / thought time and then read the text aloud and feel the silences.
- *Gesture:* accompany both individual and choral reading with gesture or facial expression or movement.

**8** Interposing:
- Interpose choral or individual reading with comment and reflection phases.
- Interpose key lines at appropriate stopping points in a recitation (for example, 'Water, water everywhere/Nor any drop to drink' in Coleridge's *The Rime of the Ancient Mariner*).
- Have everyone interpose a favourite line simultaneously to create a babble.

**9** Use of voice quality:
- whispering (loud/soft)
- raised voice
- creaky voice
- kind/unkind voice
- falsetto/bass
- vowel-less or consonant-less reading
- humming the intonation pattern but without distinct words.

## SUGGESTED TEXTS

Two poems we have found particularly good for oral reading are Peter Appleton's 'Responsibility' (see below) and, at higher intermediate and advanced levels, Wallace Stevens' 'Domination of Black' or Tennyson's choric song from 'The Lotos-Eaters'.

## RESPONSIBILITY

I am the man who gives the word,
If it should come, to use the Bomb.

I am the man who spreads the word
From him to them if it should come.

I am the man who gets the word
From him who spreads the word from him

I am the man who drops the Bomb
If ordered by the one who's heard
From him who merely spreads the word
The first one gives if it should come.

I am the man who loads the Bomb
That he must drop should orders come
From him who gets the word passed on
By one who waits to hear from *him*.

I am the man who makes the Bomb
That he must load for him to drop
If told by one who gets the word
From one who passes it from *him*.

I am the man who fills the till,
Who pays the tax, who foots the bill
That guarantees the Bomb he makes
For him to load for him to drop
If orders come from one who gets
The word passed on to him by one
Who waits to hear it from the man
Who gives the word to use the Bomb.

I am the man behind it all;
I am the one responsible.

Peter Appleton

SONG OF THE LOTOS-EATERS
There is sweet music here that softer falls
Than petals from blown roses on the grass,
Or night-dews on still waters between walls
Of shadowy granite, in a gleaming pass;
Music that gentlier on the spirit lies,
Than tired eyelids upon tired eyes;
Music that brings sweet sleep down from the blissful skies.
Here are cool mosses deep,
And through the moss the ivies creep,
And in the stream the long-leaved flowers weep,
And from the craggy ledge the poppy hangs in sleep.

Why are we weighed upon with heaviness,
And utterly consumed with sharp distress,
While all things else have rest from weariness?
All things have rest: why should we toil alone,
We only toil, who are the first of things,
And make perpetual moan,
Still from one sorrow to another thrown:
Nor ever fold our wings,
And cease from wanderings,
Nor steep our brows in slumber's holy balm;
Nor harken what the inner spirit sings,
'There is no joy but calm!'
Why should we only toil, the roof and crown of things?

Alfred Tennyson

Wherever you can, allow the students to make as many as possible of the performance decisions. If you do this, you will make them responsible for the quality of the reading and you will help them to familiarise themselves with the text and its performance requirements.

## Reading for understanding

Apart from Exercises 4.5 *Poetical chairs* and 4.10 *Key words*, all the exercises in this chapter are 'reading-for-understanding' ones. They are designed to bring learner knowledge and text together. The texts are understood because the way they are approached gives the learners the opportunity to adjust their frames of knowledge to accommodate what is new. Specifically, these exercises draw attention to the differences between everyday and literary responses (Exercises 4.2 *Asking naive questions*, 4.3 *Gossiping*, 4.4 *Relating*, 4.7 *Reflecting*), to critical reading techniques (4.6 *Improving texts*), to how dialogue and narrative blend (4.1 *Adverbs and fiction*) and to the role of context in reading for meaning (4.8 *Before and after*, 4.9 *Layers of knowledge*, 4.11 *Jigsaw reading*).

# ADVERBS AND FICTION

**4.1**

**TIME**
30 minutes

**LEVEL**
Elementary–
Intermediate

**MATERIALS**
A class set of
cards or slips of
paper each
bearing a different
sentence

One of the conventions of popular fiction in English is the use of the colourful adverb as in 'The table was *sumptuously* laid', 'The flowers drooped *despairingly*', and 'She coughed *pitifully*'. The adverb can have a lot of power in certain kinds of writing. The aim of this exercise is to give students practice in judging which adverb best highlights a verb. It is also useful in helping students understand the aspect of English humour that sees hyperbole as comic and relies on under-statement to make a point.

## Procedure

1 Hand out a different prepared sentence to each member of the group. These can be on any subject and taken from any text or just invented. Tell the students to put each sentence in inverted commas and add the phrase *he said* or *she said* to each one.
2 Ask each student to pass the sentence on to another person who must add an adverb after *said*. You may like to begin the class by writing a list of adverbs on the board, e.g. *softly, loudly, quickly*, etc.
3 Ask each person to read out their sentence, while the others make a note of the adverbs used.
4 Ask the students to pass on the sentences again, and to substitute another adverb for the first. Tell students not to use an adverb that has already been used in another sentence.
5 Ask students to read out the sentences and everyone to make a list of the adverbs used.
You can let this process go on until people run out of ideas.

### EXTENSIONS
1 After the second set of adverbs, students may find that certain characters are beginning to emerge. At this point, split the group into two or three subgroups, depending on the size of the class. Each group works on creating a dialogue, with characterisation expressed through adverbs.
2 Encourage the group to discuss the ways in which their choice of adverbs has been determined by the sex of the speaker; e.g. what is the difference between *she said sweetly* and *he said sweetly* or *she said savagely* and *he said savagely*. You may want to bring in samples of texts that use this convention heavily, such as love stories from women's magazines, to give students the chance to see how the adverb operates.
3 Ask students to substitute the verb + adverb with a single verb that they feel is synonymous, e.g. *He said loudly = he cried; she said longingly = she craved*.

## 4.2

**TIME**
15–20 minutes

**LEVEL**
Intermediate +

**SUGGESTED TEXTS**
Short story, novel, scene in a play

# ASKING NAIVE QUESTIONS

Merely seeing a literary text on a page causes us to read it in a certain, often over-respectful, way. We also know that there are some kinds of response that are usually deemed inappropriate because they appear to be insufficiently respectful. This exercise aims to practise the kinds of 'inappropriate', homely response that do not typically occur to the cultured reader.

## Procedure

1 After reading a short story, a chapter in a novel or a scene from a play, ask the students to spend five to ten minutes in silence, thinking up naive questions to put to the characters in the story or play. For example, after reading *Macbeth* Act I, scene iii, someone might want to ask the witches, 'Why don't you shave off your beards?' The more naive the questions, the better.
2 Each student reads out the most naive of their questions.

ACKNOWLEDGEMENT
This idea was sparked off by listening to Tembeka Kawa talking about teaching *Macbeth*.

## 4.3

**TIME**
30–40 minutes

**LEVEL**
Intermediate +

**MATERIALS**
A prepared list of expressions

**SUGGESTED TEXTS**
A novel or a play which the class has started to read

# GOSSIPING

Bertold Brecht complained about the spellbound way in which audiences usually watch plays in the theatre and which causes them to suspend their usual ability to make judgments. In this exercise, the class is encouraged to 'gossip' about the Hamlets and King Lears we see on the stage. The aim is to find a way of evaluating the actions of characters in a work of fiction.

## Preparation

1 Prepare a list of the kinds of expressions people use to start their sentences when they gossip about somebody else:
   • *I must say* ...
   • *There are times when* ...
   • *If it wasn't for* ...
   • *I sometimes feel* ...
   • *(S)he can be* ...
   • *I know it isn't his/her fault but*...
   • *I don't suppose*...etc.
   and write them up on the board.

2 Decide which character you want to work on from the story, chapter or scene of a play you have just read. For example, Hamlet in the play-within-the-play, or Shane in more or less any chapter of the novel of that name.

## Procedure

1 Tell the students to imagine they are one of the other characters in the story/chapter/scene; let each student choose their own character. Each student writes a short monologue expressing their feelings about the chosen character (Hamlet or Shane, for example). They can use the expressions on the board to start their sentences if it helps. Encourage them to be as colloquial and gossipy as possible.
2 Group the students by their own chosen characters (i.e. all the Claudiuses in one group, all the Ophelias in another, etc). Ask each group to choose the best monologue to read or perform to the rest of the class.

# RELATING

**4.4**

The aim of this exercise is to get the students to listen carefully to a single line of poetry and allow it to impinge on their consciousness.

**TIME**
10–15 minutes

## Procedure

**LEVEL**
Elementary +

1 After reading a poem, pair students and ask each student to identify two or three separate single lines that appeal to them.
2 When everyone has found their lines, tell the pairs to decide which of them will go first. Encourage them to look straight into each other's faces. The first speaker says one of their lines quietly and carefully. When (and only when) ready, the listener replies with 'Yes'. The first speaker then says their second line and again waits for the affirmation. When the first speaker's lines are all spoken, the roles are reversed.

### NOTE

Relating to others in the often unnatural setting of the classroom is never easy. Quite often when you try even simple relating exercises like this one, the students are embarrassed and giggle. But it is worth persevering because such activities, particularly if they become part of the regular pattern of classroom activities, deepen the students' concentration, sharpen their aesthetic awareness and help to establish a calm, orderly atmosphere.

## 4.5

**TIME**
15 minutes

**LEVEL**
Elementary +

**MATERIALS**
Each word of the
chosen text
written on a
separate piece of
paper or, ideally,
on a sticky label.
You can use large
address labels cut
into quarters

**CLASS SIZE**
Particularly
suitable for big
classes (40+)

# POETICAL CHAIRS

The aim of this exercise is to check that the students are retaining the text you are working on in their memory.

## Preparation

Choose a text that contains at least as many words as there are students in the class. A single verse of a poem you are already working with works well. Write each word on a piece of paper, or better still, on a piece of address label.

## Procedure

1 Arrange the chairs in a circle. Make sure there are exactly as many chairs in the circle as there are words in the text. Give each student a word at random and ask them to sit in the 'right' place in the circle. If you have more words than students, stick the extra words on the right chairs yourself – it is best to do this with words like *a* and *the*.
2 When the circle is complete, ask the students to work out among themselves where the line divisions come, before the poem is recited word by word round the class.

**NOTE**
This exercise works well as a way of rounding off a session in which a text has been studied. Equally, it can be used at that stage in a lesson when a text has been introduced orally and is about to be distributed in written form.

## 4.6

**TIME**
40 minutes

**LEVEL**
Intermediate +

**SUGGESTED TEXTS**
Any poem,
especially less
formal verse

# IMPROVING TEXTS

The aim of this exercise is to discover exactly how carefully a poem is written and how very difficult it is to improve the original text. This approach to a text sensitises the students to the way every chosen word relates to its phonological and semantic context.

## Procedure

1 Ask the students to work individually and allow them ten minutes to replace any five separate or consecutive words in the specified text with words or phrases of their own choice which they think will improve it.
2 Ask students to take a partner and together see if either had suggestions that really did improve the text.
3 Repeat Step 2 with pairs coming together to form fours, and then with fours coming together to make eights.
4 Any agreed improvements can be shared by the class.

Many texts are suitable for this exercise, especially less formal verse such as T S Eliot's 'Little Gidding'.

# REFLECTING

**4.7**

This exercise focuses on post-reading reflection and aims to help the students to absorb a text into their own world.

**TIME**
Depending on the length of the poem

## Procedure

1 Explain that the students are going to follow the text while you read it aloud. You will pause after each verse to allow a member of the class to make a comment. Your reading and the comment will both be recorded. Stress that all kinds of comments are acceptable: summaries, in-role improvisations, comments or questions about the poem, etc. (Alternatively, tell your class what type of comment you require.) You will expect a different student to offer a comment after each verse.

2 Start recording and read the first verse before stopping for a comment. It is a good idea to use the pause button on the cassette recorder while you wait for a comment so that you do not record the inevitable silences.

3 When you replay the tape, the class can simply listen, or there can be a discussion of the comments.

**LEVEL**
Intermediate +

**MATERIALS**
Cassette recorder

**SUGGESTED TEXTS**
Longer poems with a regular verse structure (see Suggested Texts below)

**SUGGESTED TEXTS**
Suitable texts include many ballads, such as William Morris's *The Haystack in the Floods* and *The Defence of Guinevere*, some lyrics, and longer poems like Tennyson's *The Lady of Shalott*, Keats's *La Belle Dame Sans Merci* and carefully chosen parts of Coleridge's *The Rime of the Ancient Mariner*.

## 4.8

**TIME**
40–50 minutes

**LEVEL**
Intermediate +

**REQUIREMENT**
Students will need
time to read the
text before class

**SUGGESTED
TEXTS**
Any two short
stories

# BEFORE AND AFTER

Asking students to predict the way a story will continue after reading the beginning is a well-known activity. This exercise is a more interesting variation on that theme. Further interest is added by asking a group who know the story already to set the task for their colleagues.

## Procedure

PRE-CLASS HOMEWORK

Divide the class in half and give each half a different story to read for homework. It is important that the students only read the story meant for them and that they do not discuss it with those who have not read it before they come to class.

IN CLASS

1  Divide the class into groups of seven or eight in such a way that everyone in each group has read the same story. Ask each group to agree on and write down a single sentence describing a significant incident that occurs in the middle of the story. For example, for JD Salinger's *For Esmé with Love and Squalor*, the sentence could be: 'Esmé tells the American soldier that she hopes they will meet again one day under more normal circumstances', or for Albert Camus's *The Guest*, 'So the policeman leaves the prisoner with the schoolteacher'.

2  Tell each group to swap their sentence with a group who have read the other story. Each group now tries to invent the beginning and end of the story whose middle they have just been told.

3  Have each significant sentence and story beginning and end retold before the students who have read the story reveal the authentic version.

## 4.9

**TIME**
45–50 minutes

**LEVEL**
Intermediate +

**SUGGESTED
TEXTS**
Any short poem

# LAYERS OF MEANING

This exercise is designed to enable students to see how additional pieces of information can add further layers of meaning to a text.

## Preparation

Choose a short poem, especially one with an unusual title or unexpected last line. Remove the title and writer's name. The example given here is a poem by Gerard Manley Hopkins.

I have desired to go
Where springs not fail,
To fields where flies no sharp and sided hail
And a few lilies blow.
And I have asked to be
Where no storms come,
Where the green swell is in the havens dumb,
And out of the swing of the sea.

## Procedure

1 Distribute the text and explain that if anyone knows the poem already, they should stay quiet. For the first five minutes everyone works individually writing a short paraphrase of the poem and trying to answer such questions as: 'What is this poem about? Who is speaking? What has happened to them?' It often helps to write these questions on the board.

2 Divide the class into groups of four or five. The groups have ten minutes to share their different paraphrases and agree on a spokesperson who will represent the group. The spokesperson then reads the group's collective interpretation to the rest of the class.

3 Introduce another dimension to the reading by giving the title of the poem: 'Heaven-haven'. The groups take five minutes to discuss whether this title adds anything to their reading, or changes it in any way, and then again the spokespersons report each group's views.

4 Now add the subtitle of the poem: 'A nun takes the veil'. This usually changes readings radically; most students will have followed clues of death and dying and will have to rethink their interpretation.

5 Tell the group the name of the poet, Gerard Manley Hopkins (1844-89) and give some brief information on his life and work.

6 This is a very useful activity to adapt for discussion on gender also, since the speaker in this poem is female but the poet is male. A useful comparison can be made with a poem such as Sylvia Plath's 'Gigolo' where the speaker is male but the poet is female.

## KEY WORDS

The aim of this exercise is to establish rapidly a sense of familiarity with a new text by focusing students' attention on the parts of it which they can associate with. It works best for short, simple, optimistic poems. It also works well with the first verse of 'I remember, I remember' (see page 32).

## Procedure

1 Ask the students to close their eyes and relax. They should remain like this throughout the exercise.

2 Read or recite the poem to them.

**4.10**

**TIME**
10 minutes

**LEVEL**
Beginner +

**SUGGESTED TEXTS**
Short, simple poems or a single verse of a longer poem

**3** Before reciting the poem a second time, ask the students to pick out any particular words that register strongly for them as they listen.
**4** Ask the students to mouth these words silently as you recite the poem for the third time.
**5** Ask the students to say their words aloud as you recite for the fourth time.
**6** Can the class recite the poem? If necessary, supply minimal prompting.

ACKNOWLEDGEMENT
We learnt this technique from Jim Wingate, who used it on a teacher training course at St Martin's College, Lancaster.

## 4.11

**TIME**
30 minutes

**LEVEL**
Intermediate +

**MATERIALS**
For the exercise, pieces of paper with single lines copied on them; for the variations, specially prepared handouts with half the poem copied on them

**CLASS SIZE**
Appropriate to the number of pieces in the 'jigsaw'. For the poem we have used to illustrate this exercise, at least 16 students

# JIGSAW READING

Most teachers are familiar with the jigsaw technique in which a short text is divided up into smaller units and reassembled in the correct order by the students. But in practice, it is difficult to find texts, and especially literary texts, with which this works well unless each student or group has all the pieces at the outset. Yet the best jigsaws are those where each student or group has different parts of a single text, so that negotiation must take place before the whole text can be assembled. In this exercise, our aim is to show how a well-chosen text can lead to a good jigsaw activity with lots of discussion and movement. We have chosen a question and answer poem, 'Uphill' by Christina Rossetti, because first the questions and answers can be matched, and then the whole text assembled.

UPHILL

Does the road wind uphill all the way?
　Yes, to the very end.
Will the day's journey take the whole long day?
　From morn to night, my friend.

But is there for the night a resting-place?
　A roof for when the slow, dark hours begin.
May not the darkness hide it from my face?
　You cannot miss that inn.

Shall I meet other wayfarers at night?
　Those who have gone before.
Then must I knock, or call when just in sight?
　They will not keep you waiting at that door.

Shall I find comfort, travel-sore and weak?
   Of labour you shall find the sum.
Will there be beds for me and all who seek?
   Yes, beds for all who come.

Christina Rossetti

## Preparation

Copy each line of 'Uphill' on to a separate piece of paper.

## Procedure

1 You must have at least sixteen students in the class because the poem has this number of lines. If you have more students, pair some so as to have sixteen pairs and/or individuals.
2 Distribute the separate lines and instruct the students to circulate so that the question and answer lines that match can find each other.
3 Once the questions and answers are matched, tell the students to arrange themselves in the 'correct' order. If after eight or ten minutes things do not seem to be working out, suggest that they use rhyme as an aid.

### VARIATIONS (WITH THIS TEXT)
1 Distribute a handout with just the answers and ask the students to work out and write down the questions. If you have a big class, this can be done by one part of the class whilst the rest do the exercise as described above.
2 Distribute a handout with just the questions and dictate the answers in random order. These should be written down in the appropriate places on the handout.

# CHAPTER 5

# *Translation*

The activities in this chapter continue the theme of cultural difference referred to in the Introduction (see p 10) and exemplified in exercises like 1.6 *Red Indian names* and 1.9 *Picture prompting*, but are more directly concerned with the process of interlingual and intercultural transfer. In practice, everyone translates. We all adjust our linguistic register in accordance with the situation in which we find ourselves. We take for granted the fact that the language used in a football changing room, for example, is not in the same register as the language used at an afternoon tea-party, or during a visit to our grandmother. We use language with our close friends that we do not use in formal situations. We make these adjustments almost without realising. It is when we come to interlingual translation that we start to think about the processes of transfer from one linguistic system into another, and in learning another language it is very important to be aware of those processes. We not only need to be able to translate, but we need to know how we do it. The exercises here are designed to make students aware of some of these conscious and unconscious processes. Some of the exercises work well in a multicultural classroom, whilst others, such as Exercise 5.10 *Bilingual poems*, are ideal for use in the mono-lingual classroom.

The principle behind these exercises is that translation is both dynamic and inevitable. Just as we want to get away from ideas of reading that involve a 'right' or 'wrong' way, so we also want to get away from a notion of translation that sees 'faithfulness' as good and anything less than that as bad. We do not believe that there is such a thing as a perfect translation, and so what these exercises are designed to do is to raise questions about what equivalence between languages actually means. Languages and cultures are different, and by accepting that idea of difference we can move creatively between languages, without trying to force one linguistic system into the strait-jacket of another. Exercises 5.2 *Idiotic idioms* and 5.8 *Translationese* are exercises that expose the foolishness of believing that two languages and cultures can ever be 'the same'.

# LANGUAGE AND PICTURES

This is a good exercise to use when a group is just beginning to work together as it helps people to get to know one another.

## Procedure

1 Split the students into pairs. Each pair works with a single sheet of paper and one pen. For ten minutes each pair of students communicates only by drawing pictures on their shared sheet of paper. They may not write any words on the paper and the exercise must take place in total silence.
2 When each pair has a page covered with symbols of some kind, the students each take a new sheet of paper and during the next ten minutes each one writes down what they think was communicated in Step 1.
3 In the last ten minutes each pair shares their versions of the communication. Pairs may then discuss their work with the whole group.

**5.1**

**TIME**
30 minutes

**LEVEL**
Intermediate

# IDIOTIC IDIOMS

Literal translation of idioms is always a good source of comedy for the language learner. This exercise is based on mistranslation and helps students fix idiomatic expressions in their mind. One of its aims is to raise questions about 'universal' and 'culture-bound' idioms. Another aim is to open up a discussion about equivalence in translation.

**5.2**

**TIME**
30–45 minutes

**LEVEL**
Intermediate +

## Procedure

1 Each student thinks of an idiom in their own language, which they then translate literally into English and write on a piece of paper. It is a good idea to read examples aloud to the group. For example, a literal translation of one idiom might be *as healthy as a fish* or of another *to lead a dog around a threshing floor*.
2 The papers are then passed on to the next person who has to think of an equivalent English idiom that has roughly the same meaning. For example *as healthy as a fish* might become *as fit as a fiddle*, and *to lead a dog around a threshing floor* might become *to beat around the bush*. Students may have to use dictionaries at this stage or ask you for help.

This exercise can continue until everyone has tried their hand at three or four different idioms.

## 5.3

TIME
30–45 minutes

LEVEL
Intermediate +

# INTERNATIONAL JOKES

This addresses the problem of what is and is not specifically culture-bound. It is useful in helping students to understand what constitutes comedy in different cultural contexts. It also aims to sensitise students to the problems an outsider would have in understanding their culture.

## Procedure

1 Ask everyone to think of a joke that they have heard recently in their own language and to write it down in English.
2 Each student tells their joke in turn and after each one there is a brief discussion as to whether the joke is comprehensible or not. Keep discussion to a minimum, but ask who finds the jokes funny and if not, why not.

### EXTENSION
Depending on the size of the class, one joke may occupy the whole time available. If there is additional time, or if you want to continue developing this exercise, ask students to write:
• a joke that they consider to be 'typically English'.
• a joke that they feel is universal and transcends all cultural boundaries.
Both of these extensions can produce very interesting results. In the case of the first, students have an opportunity to discuss cultural stereotypes and in the second they investigate the possibility that jokes may not be tied explicitly to a particular social group. What frequently happens is that the same joke surfaces in different cultures but related to different events or characters.

## 5.4

TIME
35 minutes

LEVEL
Elementary +

MATERIALS
A small unruled card or similarly sized piece of paper for each student

CLASS
COMPOSITION
Multicultural and multilingual

# WISE SAYINGS

Don't take the bees and the flies.
Japanese proverb

Most people can recall wise sayings in their mother tongue which are usually expressed in a pithy or idiomatic form. How do these translate into English, how can the impact of the original be retained, and in mixed nationality classes what do the students make of each other's wise sayings? One important aim of this exercise is to promote intercultural understanding by helping the students to recognise that although each of our cultures has very different ways of expressing ideas, the ideas themselves are often universal.

## Procedure

1 Arrange the students in a circle. Distribute one card or piece of paper to each student and ask them to think of a proverb in their own language and write it down.

**2** Give the students ten minutes to write a translation of their proverb on the other side of the card. Encourage the use of dictionaries and collaboration between speakers of the same mother tongue. Go round making sure that the translations are intelligible.

**3** Collect in all the cards and redistribute them round the class so that everyone gets a proverb from a foreign language. Allow several minutes for the students to prepare to read the English translations aloud in a fluent manner.

**4** Tell the students that you will read the translation on your card aloud first and that any student whose translated proverb is related to yours should read next. This process should continue without you intervening again until everyone has read their translated proverbs aloud.

**VARIATION**

For a variation suitable for higher intermediate and advanced students, see Exercise 8.11 *Proverbs of hell*.

# WORDS AND THEIR WEIGHT

One of the principal problems a language learner encounters is understanding the weight of significance attached to utterances in another language. Utterances that are polite in one language may be offensive in another, while attempts to be insulting may turn out to be ridiculous. For example, in English, 'Can you give me the salt?' is acceptable as a polite request only among close friends or family, whereas in many languages it is the equivalent of the English 'Can you pass the salt?' which is used in more formal situations.

Jenny Thomas (1983) distinguishes two types of difficulty second language learners have in this area. Quite often the same expression will have different forces in different languages, as 'Can you give me...' illustrates. The second kind of difficulty is more cultural than linguistic. When we travel to other countries we simply cannot bring ourselves to use the linguistic formulas we hear around us because they would be inappropriate in our own culture. Thus it may be perfectly polite to say 'Waiter, bring me coffee' in a particular culture, but if we are used to saying, 'Please may I have a cup of coffee', we may not be able to make the necessary cultural adjustment.

## Procedure

**1** Divide the class into groups of four or five and ask each student to think of two versions of an imaginary situation. For example, asking what is available for breakfast in either a hotel/restaurant, or in someone's home. Each student should write down what they would say in their own language and what they think they would say in English.

**5.5**

**TIME**
At least 45 minutes

**LEVEL**
Intermediate +

2 The English phrases are shared with other members of the group, and each group has to decide which two phrases are the most suitable in each situation.

3 The groups come together and share their choices. It is a good idea to have some discussion at this stage. Two things typically emerge:
  - The difference in politeness strategies between cultures: what is polite in a student's own culture may be rude in English, such as saying, 'Give me an egg' to a waiter or, 'Do you never eat eggs in this house' to your host.
  - The difficulty of sensing the effect of any unintended rudeness.

4 An interesting, optional final step is to ask the students to write couplets which compare pragmatically equivalent uses of language. For example:

'Waiter,' I said, 'bring me an egg';
'Could I possibly have an egg,' my teacher said, 'if it's not too much trouble, that is.'

It is a good idea to encourage the students to write couplets both in English and in their mother tongues.

# 5.6

**TIME**
20 minutes

**LEVEL**
Elementary +

**CLASS COMPOSITION**
Multilingual

# WHAT GETS LOST

Poetry is what gets lost in translation.
Robert Frost

The aim of this exercise is to give a sense of how exotic words can be aesthetically pleasing even when we do not know what they mean.

## Procedure

1 Ask each student to choose the two words in their mother tongues which are (a) the most beautiful and (b) the least beautiful for them, and then to translate each into English.

2 Ask the students to write the English translations on the board with 'beautiful' words on the left and 'ugly' words on the right.

3 Working in small groups, the students decide which words they would transfer to the other side of the board.

**NOTE**
This is both a fun exercise and a very thought-provoking one. It is also an exercise which promotes tolerance and understanding of the differences between one language and another and shows that aesthetic judgments are not always as predictable as we might think.

# POETRY REVERSI

The aim of this exercise is to show how difficult it is to translate a single well-known line of poetry from one's mother tongue into a second language. The exercise also shows how easily poetry 'gets lost in translation' and gives students the pleasurable, and sometimes comic, experience of reading poetry written in and translated from at least one language they do not understand.

## Preparation

Take one large sheet of coloured card for each of your students' mother tongues and one more for English. Cut out twenty 2 x 5 cm rectangles of each colour.

## Procedure

1 Group the learners by mother tongue and ask each group to recall from memory one line of poetry in their own language to work with. Do the same thing yourself for English. (John Keats's 'I have been half in love with easeful death' works well.)

2 When each group has chosen a line, ask the students to decide which colour of card will represent their language. Each group then takes enough rectangles of their colour to be able to write each word of their line on a separate one. They should use the Latin alphabet.

3 Ask the groups to translate their lines into English and to write the English translation of each word on the other side of the appropriate rectangle. This should be done as literally as possible. Sometimes one word in their language will need more than one word in English; when this happens all the English words should be written on the same rectangle. For example, *parler* (one word in French) → *to speak* (two words in English). If there is no English translation for a particular word, then nothing should be written on the English side of the rectangle. For example, in *Mach mal das Licht aus* (German for *Put the light out*) *mal* is a particle with no English equivalent. Your line should also be translated into one of the languages of the group; you may need a student to help you with this.

4 When all the translations are complete, each line should be set out on the table, English side up and in English word order, except yours which should be set out in the language it has been translated into. It is a good idea at this stage to write the name of the source language beside each line.

**EXAMPLE**

If there are three different mother tongues in the class, for example, German, Japanese and Serbo-Croat, at this stage you would have four different lines on the table:

**5.7**

**TIME**
50–60 minutes

**LEVEL**
Intermediate +

**MATERIALS**
Several large sheets of coloured card (see Preparation)

**CLASS SIZE**
The ideal class size is 8–12. There must be at least two different mother tongues in the class

*German*

| laughing | lions | must | come |

*Japanese*

| snow | mountain | snow | valley |

| snow | tree | snow | winter |

*Serbo-Croat*

| no | don't | approach | me |

| Iwant | fromfaraway | inorderthat | Ilove |

| and | Iwant | your | two |

| eyes |

*English*

| | bio | sam | napola |

| | zaljubljen | u | bezbriznu |

| smrt | (Serbo-Croat version of 'I have been half in love with easeful death') |

5 At this stage of the exercise the lines are translated back into their original languages. Each student uses their turn either to help to translate their own line back into its mother tongue or to prevent speakers of other languages from doing this to their lines by attempting a translation of the lines originating from other languages. A turn consists of saying what is written on the back of any rectangle, looking to see if it is correct and, if so, turning the rectangle over.

6 After everyone has had three or four turns, you may find it is a good idea to give each learner two turns at a time.

7 Once a line is entirely restored to its original language, it ceases to be in the game.

**NOTE**

As you do this exercise, you will find that some lines are worked on much more than others. The exercise is therefore a kind of sociolinguistic experiment in that of the three or more languages the group works with, some will become dominant and some marginalised. Which languages thrive will depend on their status as a community language (English will do well here as it will be the only common language in the group), the number of native speakers each has (if there are more southern Slavs than any other nationality in the group, Serbo-Croat will do well) and the complexity of the language itself (morphologically complex or phonetically challenging languages are not favoured). The exercise therefore teaches us something about what is necessary for a language to become a 'world' language.

ACKNOWLEDGEMENT
Margarita Pujals helped to design and pilot this exercise. The reversi element is owed to Mario Rinvolucri.

## TRANSLATIONESE

Understanding what sounds right in a language can be greatly helped if we first learn to hear what sounds wrong. This is an exercise that encourages students to pick out mistakes in English and to identify errors of style. It is also very entertaining, as so many of the mistakes are funny. Because of this comic element and also the consultation stage when students can ask each other questions, it is a good exercise for breaking down initial barriers in a group. It also aims to draw attention to the need for functional equivalence in translation and the shortcomings of translations that display only formal equivalence.

## Procedure

1 Ask the class the day before to bring a text to class. It should be in their own language, ideally a magazine or newspaper article, a tourist guide or something similar (not a literary text such as a novel or short story). Ask each student to translate about thirty lines of the text (or whatever you feel is an appropriate amount, given the time available and the level of the students) as literally as possible. Tell the students not to make any stylistic adjustments, simply to translate the text as close to word for word as possible.
2 When the translations are complete, each person quickly reads their version aloud. This generally produces some hilarious results and some examples of truly appalling English.
3 Each student passes their text on to the person sitting next to them, whose task it is to turn the piece of 'translationese' into acceptable English. Students can consult with one another and ask questions if texts are unclear.
4 If time permits, the finished version of each text can then be shared with the whole class.

### VARIATION
You can also use this exercise with literary texts, but in this case it works much better with a homogeneous language group since it is necessary to refer back to the original text in the tidying-up phase.

**5.8**

**TIME**
60 minutes

**LEVEL**
Higher
intermediate +

**MATERIALS**
None, but ask the students in advance to bring a text into class

## 5.9

**TIME**
30 minutes

**LEVEL**
Intermediate +

# CHINESE POEM

Here we use a very well-known Chinese poem but this exercise works with any similar poem. The object is twofold: students learn to build basic sentences, and they also learn about poetic language. Students are asked to build on basic images by incorporating the words of a 'literal' translation into English syntax.

## Procedure

1 Distribute copies of the basic translation. It follows the Chinese 6, 6, 6, 4, 6, syllable pattern:

MEDITATION IN AUTUMN

dry vine tree evening crow
lone hut quick stream small bridge
old road west wind lean horse
sunset suggests
to this old man his fate

Ma Chih Yuan (1250–1324)

Working independently, each member of the class writes a version of this poem in modern English. You may want to ask students to keep to the five line form, or you may allow more licence so that they do not feel they are simply imitating. Let them use as many syllables as they like but point out the syllable patterning in the Chinese version. After writing a first version, students may want to see if they can turn their poem into something shorter and more tightly structured.

2 Compare the different versions and encourage the students to concentrate on the variations. What usually happens is that students expand the basic text considerably, and there are interesting differences between the versions that include an 'I' speaker, the ones that use the third person and the ones that make the old man the speaker of the poem. This poem also enables you to introduce students to poetic conventions in English, and to the form of the elegy in particular. If there are native Chinese speakers in the class, ask them to retranslate the versions back into their own language.

# BILINGUAL POEMS

This exercise aims to make students more aware of the processes involved in bilingualism and to think also about what it is that they 'translate' as opposed to what it is that they can create directly in the new language.

## Procedure

1 Divide the students into pairs and ask them to conduct a mock interview. Each pair has to decide on the context of their interview – a classroom, with a street reporter, a job interview, a police interrogation, etc. When they have come to a decision, allow five minutes for every student to write down ten basic questions that they will ask in the interview.
2 The students then interview one another. One student asks the other the questions, and the second replies with single sentence answers. When the ten questions have been asked, the process is reversed and the second student asks the other ten questions. This takes about fifteen to twenty minutes.
3 Working separately, and using the ten basic written questions along with their recollections of the answers, each student creates a twenty-line question-and-answer poem. The only rule is that at least 50 per cent of the lines must be in English with the remainder in the student's own native language. It is up to the individual to decide on the arrangement of lines, the order of questions and answers, and the final proportion of non-English lines.

### EXTENSION

This is always a very thought-provoking exercise. There have been times when our students have been inspired to go on and create a number of bilingual poems after beginning this exercise.

Once the first poem of twenty lines has been produced, ask students to rewrite it changing the languages around, i.e. putting all English lines into their own language and vice versa. If the class shares a common language, then the pieces can be read as drama.

### SUGGESTED TEXTS

We suggest two texts as illustration: 'Address' a bilingual poem by Alurista, the Mexican–American poet (see overleaf), and 'What Were They Like?', a bicultural question-and-answer poem by Denise Levertov. If the class has worked with these texts earlier, this may help the writing process here.

**5.10**

**TIME**
60 minutes

**LEVEL**
Higher
intermediate +

LANGUAGE THROUGH LITERATURE

## ADDRESS

address
occupation
age
marital status
– perdone...
      yo me llamo pedro
telephone
height
hobbies
previous employers
– perdone...
      yo me llamo pedro
pedro ortega
zip code
i.d. number
classification
rank
– perdone mi padre era
    el señor ortega
    (a veces don josé)
race

Alurista

# CHAPTER 6

# Writing

In traditional literature teaching, the most neglected area of all is writing. Students are taught about reading and taught also to revere the opinions of literary critics, but they are rarely taught to write anything except essays. Yet it is only comparatively recently that the separation of reading, criticism and writing has happened. The great scholar critics of the nineteenth century wrote poetry themselves and so were in a better position to criticise the work of other poets. In the twentieth century the gap between talking about literature and producing it has been steadily widening, and we believe that this has all kinds of negative effects, not least of which is the spread of the 'lit-crit' industry, wherein critics pontificate about poems without ever having so much as tried to write a poem themselves.

The exercises in this section are designed to help students increase their linguistic skills by writing creatively in various ways. We have included exercises that involve poetry, prose, dialogue, and drama, besides exercises in characterisation, sound patterning and shape. Several of them involve students in using their own lives as raw material – Exercises 6.4 *Autobiography in objects* and 6.6 *Writing about work* enable students to utilise their own inner resources. We have often found that students can continue to develop these exercises in all sorts of ways once the course comes to an end.

## SHAPE POEMS

Poems that make shapes have been in vogue from time to time. Once you have the theme, which is usually given by the outline, they are relatively easy to write because the syntactic and cohesive requirements are often more relaxed than in a conventional poem laid out in a linear sequence. For this reason, this exercise is particularly suitable for poem-making in a second language and aims to give the students confidence in the first steps of assembling the words necessary to make a poetic text.

## Preparation

Choose twelve to fifteen different magazine pictures that each have a distinctive outline and that will produce reasonable quality photocopies. The subject matter can be almost anything: faces, countries and continents, hot air balloons, trees, aeroplanes, trains, flowers,

**6.1**

**TIME**
25 minutes

**LEVEL**
Higher
elementary +

**MATERIALS**
A good supply of
magazine
pictures, scissors;
access to a photo-
copier

food, animals, etc. Cut the pictures out and discard the backgrounds in which they were set. As each student will choose one outline, make enough photocopies for the students to have plenty of choice.

## Procedure

Ask each student to choose a photocopy and write a poem around the outline. Explain that good poems of this kind often consist of sequences of phrases rather than whole sentences and may also contain the same word(s) repeated a number of times. Some students will follow the outlines more faithfully than others – this does not matter.

### FOLLOW-UP
This exercise can be a preliminary to reading a shape poem.

### VARIATION
It is also possible to supply students with shape outlines drawn on sheets of paper. Although this is easier to organise, the results tend to be less interesting because students are merely writing round an outline rather than studying a picture first and then writing round the outline. Here are some outlines to photocopy and enlarge:

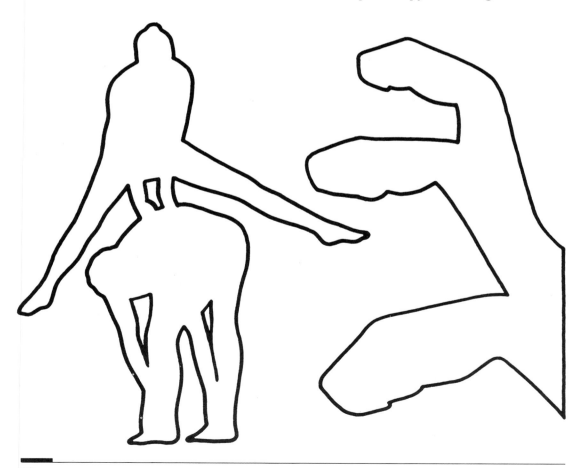

## 6.2

**TIME**
30 minutes

**LEVEL**
Higher
elementary +

**MATERIALS**
A variety of
different small
objects such as
flowers, leaves,
litter, stones, toys,
edibles, children's
bedroom detritus,
etc. in a carrier
bag

# MY POEM IS ME

My taste was me.
Gerard Manley Hopkins

The aim of this exercise is to break up the process of writing a poem into two stages, first collecting and then shaping the language needed.

## Preparation

Take at least twice as many small objects to class as there are students.

## Procedure

1 Take the objects to class in a carrier bag and begin by tipping them out on to the floor in the middle of the room. Ask each student to choose one.
2 Each student should spend five minutes considering how their object reflects their personality. It is surprising how easily the ideas come. Then suggest that the students start to write down all the ideas that occurred to them and all those that are still coming. Allow a further five to ten minutes.
3 Tell the students to write a poem entitled 'Me' made up of selected fragments from their notes joined together in whatever ways seem appropriate.
4 Those who wish to share their poems can read them aloud.

ACKNOWLEDGEMENT
This is a variation on Judith Baker's idea for teacher training courses at Pilgrims. She gets the trainees to choose a button and then think of all the ways their chosen button reflects their approach to teaching.

## 6.3

**TIME**
30 minutes

**LEVEL**
Higher
elementary +

# FRAMES

Asking students to recall their experience in a structured way and then to write a collective poem using this resource is a well-established technique. It combines many good principles: the subject matter is learner-centred and person-related, the writing is collaborative and the responsibility thus a shared one, and the effect of the whole greater than the sum of its parts. As with many of these exercises, one important aim of this exercise is to surprise students with the quality of what they can produce.

## Procedure

1 The students should work in groups of six to eight. Use a visualisation exercise (see page 38) to get the students to recall the thoughts

they have as they lie in bed at the end of the day waiting for sleep to come.

2 As they come out of the visualisation, ask each student to write down four or five of these images or ideas in one of the following forms:

   a) the (noun) of . . .

   b) the (noun) that/who . . .

     (for example, 'the laughter of Maria' or 'the man who cuddled his child').

It is best if each image or idea is written on a separate small piece of paper.

3 Ask each group to arrange some or all of these in a suitable order after these opening lines (or your own variation on them):

At the end of the day as I lie waiting for sleep to come
These pass through my drowsy mind:

## VARIATIONS

Endless variations are easy to think of. They may be variations on:

1 The form of words in which the images or ideas are recorded.
For example, you could ask for:
  • adjective + noun combinations.
  • two syllables + two syllables or three syllables + three syllables.
  • words beginning with sibilants (or labials), etc.

2 The context which stimulates the reactions. For example, instead of focusing the visualisation on the moments before sleep, you could focus it on:
  • views (from a bridge, a mountain top, an aeroplane).
  • sounds (of summer, a sporting event, a storm).
  • memories (of childhood, the seaside, grandparents), etc.

# AUTOBIOGRAPHY IN OBJECTS

**6.4**

This exercise is designed to help students write about themselves by breaking down feelings of self-consciousness that often arise when the blunt instruction 'Write about yourself' is given by a teacher.

**TIME**
30–40 minutes

**LEVEL**
Higher
elementary +

## Procedure

1 Ask each member of the class to choose six objects that they have brought with them into the classroom. Particularly common are pens, pencils, shoes, items of jewelry, money, purses, etc. Give them five minutes to arrange these six objects into a meaningful form on the desk/floor in front of them. This must be done in complete silence.

2 When they have finished, give the students a further five minutes to walk round the room, also in complete silence, looking at everyone

else's objects. It is very important that nobody speaks in this time, because this is an activity designed to stimulate unconscious processes and the effect will be destroyed if anyone starts asking questions or giving explanations.

3 Ask the students to return to their places, to look again at their own arrangements and to write a biographical description of the arranger using the third person, e.g. 'He/She is a disorganised character who has forgotten to clean his/her shoes'. This stage of the exercise often produces interesting results. Some people write very funny self-portraits, some write recognisable autobiographies and others write completely fictitious biographies. The process of arranging the objects and then comparing the arrangements triggers off all sorts of new associations. The time you spend on this stage of the activity will vary according to the linguistic competence of the class.

4 At the end of the session ask the group to read out their (auto) biographies.

ACKNOWLEDGEMENT
The idea for this activity came from Sue Jennings's work in drama-therapy.

## 6.5

**TIME**
20–30 minutes

**LEVEL**
Intermediate +

## SOUNDS OF WORDS

The aim of this exercise is to provide a sequence of words linked by sounds as a preparation for writing.

## Procedure

Three different procedures are possible for this exercise:

**VARIATIONS**
1 The class sits in a circle. Start with a single word and let the exercise run clockwise around the circle. Each person says a word that is linked to the previous word, not by meaning but by sound; e.g. *nice–rice–twice–surprise* or *black–blinkered–blessing–dressing*. Variations in what students understand by sound links will be considerable.

2 The class sits in a circle and another word is passed around. This time each student says a word that is connected to that initial word by sound, e.g. *water–dripping–river–wave–flow*, etc. Keep introducing new words whenever everyone has had a turn with the initial word.

3 Give each student a different word and ask them to write down as many words linked to that initial one by sound as they can think of. Then ask them to write a short prose passage or ten lines of free verse using the words on their list.

# WRITING ABOUT WORK

**TIME**
60 minutes

**LEVEL**
Advanced

This exercise works best with adults, especially with a group where there is range of different occupations. Describing your work to someone who is not a specialist can be difficult. Detailed knowledge of how machinery functions or how committee structures operate can result in a language that is understandable only to those people involved in the same work. When it is necessary to describe a kind of work, either for professional reasons or because a character in a piece of prose fiction is involved in doing it (cf. D H Lawrence or Sid Chaplin's mining stories, university novels, sea-faring novels etc.) then the student may experience difficulty. This exercise tackles the problem of specialised language use and reader-comprehension. It is based on film techniques of slow motion and fast forward. Its aim is to show how one can write in a way that one thinks is clear, only to find that a reader may not understand it. It works well with mature students who have spent a lot of time outside educational institutions.

## Procedure

1 Tell the students to describe in as much detail as possible a simple activity such as picking up a cup and drinking from it or sitting down in a chair. The aim here is to slow down students' thought processes and to write at length about an action that only takes a few seconds to perform. Allow about ten minutes for this first stage.

2 Now students have to accelerate. They write an account of a morning's work in a factory, shop, or office, at home, in a library, etc. in ten minutes. Remind students that they must write as though they were writing for fellow workers who understand exactly what the work consists of and who understand all specialist terminology.

3 Divide the class into groups of three or four people who share with one another the work written about in Step 2. At this point you may be able to show how in some cases the account of the morning's work is incomprehensible to outsiders. Take about ten to fifteen minutes for discussion.

4 Students rewrite their account of the morning's work to take into consideration the problems experienced by members of the group who have failed to grasp the full significance of what the writer has tried to say. This step involves the 'translation' of specialist language into accessible language. Ask the groups to discuss the revised versions and decide whether a degree of incomprehensibility (i.e. terminology that is technical and does not necessarily need to be fully understood by everyone) is acceptable or not.

**VARIATION**
You can adapt this exercise to help students describe very specific cultural contexts, e.g. a morning's work in an African village, where readers may not understand information about customs, plants, food, etc. without some kind of explanation.

## 6.7

**TIME**
60 minutes

**LEVEL**
Intermediate +

# COMIC OR TRAGIC?

This exercise enables students to try their hand at writing in two opposite ways. It is also helpful in writing dialogue. When the dialogues are read aloud, the activity can also help students to understand how the comic and the tragic are interpreted differently in different cultural contexts.

## Procedure

1 Briefly outline a situation, for example, a husband or wife comes home and finds their partner in a compromising situation with someone else. Working either individually or in pairs, the students then write the dialogue that takes place between husband and wife. They must produce a minimum of twenty lines. Warn them not to write anything but dialogue (i.e. no authorial comment and no stage directions). The only other rule is that their dialogue must be either comic or tragic. It is important to allow them enough time to think about the task. You might want to set this exercise the day before to allow students to prepare for it thoroughly, or to begin the writing process before coming to class.

2 Vary the time allotted according to the skills of the group. Then when time is up, ask each pair to read out their dialogue, and ask the others to guess which is tragic and which is comic. This exercise usually produces quite unexpected results. Often one person's tragedy is another person's comedy and vice versa.

### EXTENSIONS

1 The basic exercise can be used as the first step in building a group playlet. You could 'stage' the dialogues, with pairs of students reading each one in turn. Later, ask the students to add stage directions, which will require them to consider carefully what those directions actually do, and how they are constructed.

2 Ask students to insert the dialogue into a third-person narrative which frames it and so alters the impact of the direct speech.

3 Ask students to create a variation that examines questions of gender and language by changing the sex of the speakers in the narrative, giving 'his' lines to 'her' and vice versa. Students then discuss whether this gender reversal works and if not, why not.

# OBJECT AND CHARACTER

**6.8**

This exercise is very good for introducing members of a class to one another. Either prepare it in advance, by asking students to bring an object into the classroom, or make it impromptu by asking everyone to use an object that they have in their possession at the time. The aim is to provide a step-by-step process by which students can experiment with creating a character. This exercise works very well if scheduled just before a lunch break or at the end of the day's work, because often students find so much to talk about that they want to continue discussing the two creative processes they each encounter – their own and that of the person who has worked with their object.

**TIME**
At least 45 minutes

**LEVEL**
Intermediate +

**MATERIALS**
Each member of the class brings in an object of their own choice

## Procedure

1   If possible the class sits in a circle. Ask everyone to come forward and place their object in the centre of the circle on the floor (or on the front desk if the group is not seated in a circle).

2   i Tell each student to go and pick up a different object and return to their own place. Allow five minutes for the students to handle the objects in silence and to write down any thoughts that occur to them during this period.

   ii Then ask them to imagine an owner of the object. Allow another ten to fifteen minutes for writing notes on the character of this imaginary person.

   iii Finally, in a further ten minutes ask them to write a description of the character.

3   Then tell the class to find the person who was written about their object. Ask everyone to get up and move about the room. Each student should meet two people  – the owner of the object they have written about and the person who has written about the object they originally put in the circle. Of course this means that people will have to mill around, finding the ones they want to talk to and in turn being interrupted by others wanting to talk to them. This meeting time is often very noisy but it is important that it should take place. It is a good idea to allow ten minutes at least for this meeting and for people to discuss the characters they have created.

### EXTENSIONS

1 Ask the students to give a name to their character, or to place them in a story, or to work with someone else in the group and to bring two characters together.

2 This exercise can be used as a basis for drama. Ask the students to walk like their character, to carry out designated tasks as their character (for example, how would your character clean a floor? dance the tango? push to the front of a queue? etc) and eventually give their character dialogue.

## 6.9

**TIME**
60 minutes

**LEVEL**
Intermediate +

# THREE WISHES

This exercise makes a good starting point for an activity in characteri-sation. It can also provide the first of a series of building blocks in creating a piece of extended work.

## Procedure

1 Ask each student to take three pieces of paper. On the first everyone should write: 'I wish I were . . .'. On the second they should write 'I wish I had . . .' and on the third 'I wish I could . . .'. When they have finished, tell them to complete the sentences, writing whatever they like.
2 Ask them to place each piece of paper on the front desk or on the floor in three separate piles, one for each sentence group: *Were; Had; Could*. Shuffle the piles and tell each student to take one from each pile.
3 This step lasts approximately fifteen minutes. Ask each student to read through the sentences and then write their own impression of the character of the person that emerges from their reading. The wishes might be fantastical, for example, or materialistic, or a mix-ture of both. The task of each student is to imagine a character who might have expressed three such wishes and to write a sketch of that imaginary person.
4 Ask the students to share their portraits with the whole class.

### EXTENSION
Develop the character further. Ask students to locate their characters in a story, for example, by imagining what could happen if any (or all) of the wishes came true.

## 6.10

**TIME**
30–40 minutes

**LEVEL**
Intermediate +

**MATERIALS**
One small piece of card for each student

# GENRES

Collaborative story writing is a well-known activity. This version of Barry Palmer's, in which each group creates a parody of a genre, makes an ideal accompaniment to reading a story or novel in the genre parodied. The aim of the exercise is therefore to give an insight into the typical features of a story genre.

## Procedure

1 Arrange the students in groups of seven sitting in circles. Groups with odd numbers are essential, so be prepared to join a group yourself. Where seven is impossible, five or nine can also work.
2 Either tell each group what sort of story to write or allow each group to choose. Possible genres include romance, fairy story, detective story, spy story/thriller, western, folk tale, science fiction, travel/ exploration, children's stories.

**3** When a group has decided on its genre, each student:
  **i** takes a small piece of card and writes down a typical word they would expect to find in such a story (for example, *bloodstain* for a detective story or *moonlight* for a romance),
  **ii** writes their first sentence of such a story on a sheet of paper. This sentence must include the chosen word.
**4** When everyone in the group has written their sentence, each card is passed one place to the left and each sheet of paper one place to the right. Each student then adds another sentence to the story on the sheet in front of them, this time incorporating the word on the card that has been passed to them. Continue repeating this step.
**5** Remind groups that the seventh sentence will be the final one and that it should therefore be a conclusion of some kind.
**6** After the seventh sentence has been written, the stories and cards should be passed one more place round the circle so that they are back with the writers of the first sentences. Each student can now read their completed story aloud.

**NOTE**
This exercise gets more difficult as it progresses and as each new sentence has more preceding text to relate to. The final reading activity is particularly interesting as the participants listen for the way the key words are used.

ACKNOWLEDGEMENT
This is Barry Palmer's idea from a DUET Workshop in Klagenfurt.

# FIFTY-WORD NOVEL

**6.11**

**TIME**
15–20 minutes

**LEVEL**
Intermediate +

This exercise can be used to encourage students either to read or to write. It offers a way of helping them tackle long prose works in English (you might ask them specifically to write a Dickens novel in fifty words) or as a way of helping them shape their thoughts concisely and create new material to use later on.

## Procedure

Ask students to use no more than fifty words to give a plot summary of a novel. Either ask them to summarise a novel they have read, in which case when they read their pieces aloud, the rest of the class has to try and guess what it is, or ask them to write an original fifty-word novel. The only other rules are that there must be a beginning and an end, and the fifty words cannot be used just to start a plot and leave it unfinished.

**EXTENSION**
The fifty-word novels make ideal material for merging texts. Ask students to work in pairs, putting their two fifty-word novels together to make a ninety- or one hundred-word epic.

## 6.12

**TIME**
40–60 minutes

**LEVEL**
Intermediate +

**MATERIALS**
A bag of objects, which can be randomly selected or group specific, e.g. stones. Prepare the bag before the class begins

# SYLLABLE POEMS

This exercise can be treated as complete in itself or can be the first stage in a series of steps teaching students about the nature of English poetry. It takes students away from the more traditional still-life descriptive ways of making a poem by defamiliarising the object in question and it also makes them aware of the way in which syllabic patterns work in English.

## Procedure

1 Take the bag of objects round to each student and invite them to put their hand in and take one object out.
2 This next stage must be carefully timed. Allow ten minutes exactly. Invite each student to experience the object in complete silence and by using all five senses in turn. So if they have a stone, they should look at it, taste it, smell it, listen to it, feel it. Inevitably some senses become more or less important at this stage. While they are going through this process, tell the students to write down any words that come into their heads on a sheet of paper. They do not have to shape these words into phrases or sentences.
3 When the ten-minute period is over, tell the students they are going to write a poem about their object, following these rules:
   i There can be only two lines.
   ii The first line must contain exactly ten syllables.
   iii The second line must contain exactly seven syllables.
   iv Students must only use the words they wrote down in Step 2.
   It is important to explain to students that there is a difference between counting syllables in spoken and written English. A word such as 'business' can either be reckoned as having two or three syllables, depending on whether the student considers its pronunciation (two syllables) or its division on the page (three syllables). They can choose whether to count the syllables in either the spoken or written words.
4 Ask the students to read their poems to the class. This exercise often produces quite beautiful results with students surprised at what they have created.

**EXTENSIONS**
1 In advanced classes you can take this exercise much further. After the syllable poem, ask students to use their word list with slight additions to make a rhymed couplet. Then ask them to write a four-line rhyming stanza, which always seems much easier than it actually is and teaches a lot about rhyme in English verse.
2 Ask students to write six lines of free verse. What happens by now, of course, is that they can recognise that free verse in English is by no means free, and so this stage is much more complex than if they had

begun by writing free verse about their object. (Free verse: verse whose metrical and/or rhyme patterns are irregular.)

3 You can continue through other verse forms. Terza rima works well, and since this form has been revived by many contemporary poets it is useful to try it out. (Terza rima: three-line verses of five iambic feet plus one extra eleventh syllable with the middle line of each verse rhyming with the first and third lines of the next verse.) Eventually, with a long session of at least two hours and an advanced class working very hard, it is possible to ask students to try their hand at writing a sonnet.

# CLONING WITH A DIFFERENCE

At elementary levels, the teaching of writing often takes the form of a copying exercise of some kind. This exercise is based on a sophisticated version of the copying idea. One aim of the exercise is to demonstrate how easy it can be to write a poem which says something true, deep and private.

## Preparation

Photocopy a short poem (sonnet length is ideal) so that it is printed in the bottom left-hand corner of a sheet of A4. The level and age range of the class will determine the choice of text and the type of instructions you give in class. Here we exemplify with W B Yeats's 'When You Are Old', a text chosen for adults at higher intermediate or advanced level.

### 6.13

**TIME**
The last 10 minutes of a session

**LEVEL**
Intermediate +

**MATERIALS**
Photocopies of a short poem (see Preparation)

### WHEN YOU ARE OLD

When you are old and grey and full of sleep,
And nodding by the fire, take down this book,
And slowly read, and dream of the soft look
Your eyes had once, and of their shadows deep;

How many loved your moments of glad grace,
And loved your beauty with love false or true,
But one man loved the pilgrim soul in you,
And loved the sorrows of your changing face;

And bending down beside the glowing bars,
Murmur, a little sadly, how Love fled
And paced upon the mountains overhead
And hid his face amid a crowd of stars.

W B Yeats

## Procedure

1 Ask the students to think of the name of someone for whom they once had very strong feelings, even if the person concerned did not know about these feelings. Check that everyone has a name in mind.

2 Distribute the handout with 'When You Are Old' in the bottom left-hand corner and instruct each student to copy the opening words 'When you are old and grey', to follow them with the name of the friend, and continue copying out as fast as possible and making whatever small changes are appropriate.

3 Because of their subject matter these poems should not be read aloud. Where the institution permits, allow each person (including yourself) to leave quietly when their writing is done. With a different subject, the students could share their writing in small groups.

## 6.14

**TIME**
10–15 minutes

**LEVEL**
Beginner +

**SUGGESTED TEXTS**
Simple single lines of poetry containing the word *I*

# WRITING FROM STARTERS

This exercise demonstrates how several plain statements with a shared form, when taken together, amount to very much more than the sum of their parts. And because the form is shared with a famous poet, the sense of achievement is greatly heightened.

## Preparation

Select a line from a poem you are going to read in class. The line should start with four or five simple words, one of which must be *I*.

## Procedure

1 Dictate the opening words of the line and ask each student to complete it with something true to their own experience or feelings. If you were working with John Keats's 'I have been half in love with easeful death', for example, you would dictate just 'I have been . . .'.

2 Have all the students read the lines out loud one by one, with yourself reading the original one last of all. (With classes larger than about twelve, it is best to divide into smaller groups and read your line as the final one of each group – thus the students write 'verses'.) It often works well to repeat the reading a second time, trying to achieve a more uniform, more poetic presentation.

3 Discuss the line you read before reading the text from which it was taken.

## SUGGESTED TEXTS
Suitably prosaic starters include:

- I was a (traveller then upon the moor)
  William Wordsworth, 'Resolution and Independence'

- I know that I shall (meet my fate)
  W B Yeats, 'An Irish Airman Forsees his Death'

- I hope to (see my Pilot face to face)
  Alfred Tennyson, 'Crossing the Bar'

- I have been (half in love with easeful death)
  John Keats, 'Ode to a Nightingale'

It is easy to find them dozing in most of the best-known poems.

### NOTES
1 If you were working with a class of 100, this exercise would enable each member of the class to contribute in just six minutes.
2 This exercise makes a nice start or finish to a lesson even when you do not want to read the poem from which the line is taken. The texts suggested above work well for this purpose.

# NEWSPAPER POETRY

This exercise works on two levels:
- It helps students to shape a piece of free verse out of very straight-forward, everyday language (the opposite of what many imagine to be flowery and 'poetic').
- It also teaches students about wordplay in English. It is both a language learning activity and a lesson on how to read and structure a poem. It is useful for introducing discussions and further work on ideology and language.

## Preparation

Select short passages from any newspaper for each student. They must be in very straightforward language, and so it is a good idea to choose material from local or evening papers rather than from large national dailies.

## Procedure

1 Give each student a cutting and ask them to read through the passage, underlining words and phrases that strike them as signifi-cant. The decision as to what constitutes significance is left to each individual – some people may underline words they do not know,

**6.15**

**TIME**
30–40 minutes +
30 minutes for
optional further
stage

**LEVEL**
Intermediate +

**SUGGESTED
TEXTS**
Several short
passages from a
newspaper

words they are fond of, words they dislike, words that seem important to the news item, words that are comical, etc. Each student should underline ten words, excluding articles and conjunctions.

2 Ask each student to arrange their ten words into a new order. They may add articles and prepositions and change the tense of verbs, and must set the words out in separate lines.

### EXAMPLE

Given the following passage, a student might underline these words:

Ghetto-blasters which deafen passengers on coaches and buses are being outlawed. From next month, people whose portable radios or cassette players blare out face arrest and fines up to £400. Regulations to clamp down on loud music on beaches and trains may also be introduced. Under the bus and coach law, a passenger annoyed by a persistent ghetto-blaster can get the driver or conductor to ask the offender to turn it down. If the noise continues the vehicle can be driven to the nearest police station – or stopped alongside a police officer – and the offender arrested.

This could result in the following:

Outlawed music
blares from the ghetto
police clamp down
Arrest the music!
Stop the offenders!
Music
     stops.

One interesting aspect of this exercise is that by isolating words and then reshaping them into free verse, a very different point of view often emerges, as shown by the above example.

### EXTENSION

This exercise also works in reverse. Once they have written their poems ask each student to pass theirs on to the next person, who then writes what they imagine was the original piece in the newspaper.

Finally, ask all the students to exchange information on the shaping processes that have taken place as words move out of their original context, are placed in a new order that creates a new meaning and are then recontextualised by someone else with no knowledge of the starting point.

# COMPOSITE POEMS

This exercise shows how, once we have a model, the tone, prosody and lexis are often less difficult to reproduce than we would imagine.

## Preparation

Ask each student to bring ten separate lines of English verse to class, each written on a different small piece of paper. They may be chosen from one poem or from several different poems.

## Procedure

1 Sitting in groups of eight, the students pool all their lines and try to arrange them into eight different groups, each of which has something in common, for example, theme, tone, rhythm. (If you have a group of seven, they must make seven groups of lines, etc.)

   Tip: It is easier to work if you allow the students to get up and walk around their table – otherwise only some of the group can see what is going on. Allow each group as long as it takes to complete this phase – they may need as long as fifteen minutes.

2 Instruct each student to take one group of lines and lay them out on the table, leaving a one-line space between each. They should be laid out in an order that allows the student to make a poem out of them by writing their own lines in between. Once each student has an idea for writing a poem, then they can take pen and paper and start writing.

3 Once everyone in the group has finished writing, members of the group read their poems to each other.

**6.16**

**TIME**
Pre-class preparation and 45 minutes in class

**LEVEL**
Higher intermediate +

**MATERIALS**
Students each bring 10 separate lines of English verse to class

# DRAMA AS SPEECH ACT

Speech Act theory distinguishes between the propositions or ideas that sentences contain and what these same sentences actually count as doing when they are uttered. So 'It's you again!' contains the proposition that the addressee has returned to a place he or she was in formerly but conveys the message that the speaker is irritated. And perhaps surprisingly, 'It's me again!' conveys the quite different message that the speaker is apologising for being a nuisance.

Drama is obviously built around speech acts rather than propositional truth: that is to say, it is not so much the literal meanings of the sentences that are important as what the speaker intends to achieve by stating them. This is especially true in contemporary drama.

The aim of this exercise is to raise the students' awareness of the importance of this area of language in understanding contemporary

**6.17**

**TIME**
40 minutes

**LEVEL**
Intermediate +

**SUGGESTED TEXTS**
A short, pithy exchange from a novel or contemporary play

drama. It is an area of particular difficulty for non-native speakers since, although the meaning of the propositions may be clear, what the utterances actually count as doing is often difficult to guess at.

## Preparation

Choose a short, pithy exchange between two characters from a contemporary drama in which the speech acts are more important that the propositional meaning. (We have chosen the opening of Act II of Harold Pinter's *The Caretaker* to illustrate this exercise.)

*A few seconds later.*
   MICK *is seated,* DAVIES *on the floor, half seated, crouched.*
   *Silence.*
MICK. Well?
DAVIES. Nothing, nothing. Nothing.
   *A drip sounds in the bucket overhead. They look up.* MICK
   *looks back to* DAVIES.
MICK. What's your name?
DAVIES. I don't know you. I don't know who you are.
   *Pause.*
MICK. Eh?
DAVIES. Jenkins.
MICK. Jenkins?
DAVIES. Yes.
MICK. Jen . . . kins.
   *Pause.*
      You sleep here last night?
DAVIES. Yes.
MICK. Sleep well?
DAVIES. Yes.
MICK. I'm awfully glad. It's awfully nice to meet you.
   *Pause.*
      What did you say your name was?
DAVIES. Jenkins.
MICK. I beg your pardon?
DAVIES. Jenkins!
   *Pause.*

List all the words used in alphabetical order. In the opening of Act II, the first four exchanges (i.e. eight utterances) contain the following words:

| | | | | |
|---|---|---|---|---|
| are | don't | eh | I | Jenkins |
| know | name | nothing | well | what's |
| who | yes | you | your | |

The next four exchanges repeat some of the words in the original list and also add:

| | | | | |
|---|---|---|---|---|
| awfully | beg | did | glad | here |
| I'm | it's | last | meet | nice |
| night | pardon | say | sleep | to |
| was | what | | | |

Write each of these lists on the board.

## Procedure

1 Ask the students to work in pairs. Each pair constructs a four-exchange dialogue (Speaker A, Speaker B, x 4) between two imaginary people using only the words in the first list. The words may be used more than once and it is not necessary for every word to be used, but no other words at all may be introduced. Advise the students that it is best to begin by deciding on the characters and their relationship to each other before starting to write.

2 Ask the students to write a further four exchanges in the same conversation adding the words in the second list. They may use words from either list as often as they wish at this stage.

3 Ask pairs to read or act out their dialogues.

4 Distribute the original text from which the words were taken for reading/discussion.

**VARIATION**

This writing exercise also makes a good homework activity.

# CHAPTER 7

# *Beginners*

The exercises in this chapter are for beginners, although not of course for beginners in their first English lesson. But within only a few lessons of starting English classes, these exercises begin to come within the learner's reach.

There are three kinds of reasons for using literature with early-stage learners. We have discussed one of these reasons in the Introduction (see pages 7 – 8) where we observed that in the early stages of first language acquisition children play with and explore poetic arrangements. One might add here that everyone knows this is true of first language acquisition, as the extensive literature of 'nursery rhymes' and songs that exists in most cultures attests. We went on to argue that in the early stages of second language acquisition too 'the music of language', as Gattegno (1972, 1976) calls it, is very consciously felt, and the natural harmonies of the language are actually more accessible than in later stages of learning.

The second reason for using literature in the early stages of language learning is to do with creativity. Our approach to literature, which places a strong emphasis on the importance of literary practice, is to do with *making* things. The word *poet* itself comes from the Greek word meaning *to make*. It is very important to provide beginners with the pleasure of making and exploring aesthetically satisfying patterns. It is equally important to help them to shape their natural creativity and give it an acceptable form.

And thirdly, we want to challenge the assumption that beginners cannot work with literature simply because of their language level. It is a rare, but in our view very rewarding, experience to teach mixed-ability groups across the whole range from beginner to advanced. One of us does this sort of teaching fairly regularly and has found that it is an eye-opening experience to sit down and make a list of all the things beginners and advanced students can do equally well. We hope that when you try the exercises in this chapter, you will be convinced that working with literature can also be included in the list of things that both beginners and advanced students, in their own ways and at their own levels, can do equally well.

What then is a beginner's exercise? Conventional beginner and elementary writing exercises often consist of little more than copying texts, perhaps occasionally with minor changes or by collating from more than one source. We think that more creative, genuine writing is possible at this level and particularly poetic writing because sentence structure and logical argumentation are frequently de-emphasised in poetry. Literature is to do with combining phonetic segments and with combining words, not necessarily always according to standard semantic and syntactic criteria. For this reason, learner-provided combinations of sounds may often be literary, as in exercises such as 7.1 *Sounds* or 7.3 *Rhymes* or 7.5 *Likeness*. In 2.12 *Substituting* and 2.15 *Replacing* in Chapter 2 and in Exercise 7.7 *Words that fit* in this chapter, we show how the vocabulary of literary texts lends itself well to the substitution of single words on poetic criteria. For learners still at the stage where making complete sentences is too difficult, intervening in this way in literary texts is satisfying, raises awareness of the phonetic, semantic, pragmatic and syntactic properties of individual words and produces real results that would not be achievable unless the text were a poem.

Finally, this chapter provides only a few ideas to get you started on working with beginners. We hope that it will inspire you to think of lots of new and better ideas of your own.

# SOUNDS

Most native speakers of English will have played 'Constantinople' as children. This is 'Constantinople' with a poetic follow-up which aims to raise the students' awareness of the innate aesthetic qualities of certain sound sequences.

## Procedure

1 The students may work individually or in pairs. Ask them to make fifty words out of any combination of the letters that occur in the word *Constantinople*. Two-thirds of the words should be in English and one-third in their own language. Allow fifteen to twenty minutes for this.
2 Tell the students to circle as many of the words in their lists as sound poetic to them.
3 Go round the class several times, with each person saying one of their words aloud until all the circled words have been spoken aloud.

### EXTENSION
If you wish, the poetic words can serve as the basis for writing a short poem.

### ACKNOWLEDGEMENT
Margareta Olufsson suggested allowing mother-tongue items in this exercise, which improves our idea immeasurably.

**7.1**

**TIME**
40 minutes

**LEVEL**
Beginner/
Elementary

## 7.2

**TIME**
40 minutes

**LEVEL**
Beginner/
Elementary

# WORDS

This is a very simple exercise that gradually increases in difficulty as it progresses. It is based on a children's game and its simplicity helps to build students' confidence in the early stages of a beginners course. It also aims to give the students a first sense of how a few words with the same initial letter can be presented almost as a poem.

## Procedure

1 The students sit in a circle. Write the letters of the English alphabet on the board.
2 Choose one person to start, and ask them to say a word beginning with A. The person on their right then says a word beginning with B and so on. Once Z is reached, the next person starts again with A and continues through the alphabet. If at any time a student cannot think of a word, then they drop out. This continues until everyone is out or until you decide the time is up.
3 Anyone who has dropped out then has to write down five words beginning with the letter they missed. So, for example, if a student dropped out because they could not think of a word beginning with E, they must find five words that all begin with E.
4 Each student then reads their five words out, but in an evenly spaced tempo. Ask them to savour the sounds and allow time for each word to be appreciated.

### EXTENSION
Give out another starting word, then ask students to go round the circle finding words that begin with the first two letters of the initial word, e.g. *animal, answer, antelope, angry*. Now ask students to go round again finding words that begin with the first three letters of the initial word, e.g. *bargain, barnyard, barley, barely*. You can continue with four letters. When almost everyone is out, allow a final round with dictionaries.

### VARIATION
Ask students to think in terms of categories, such as animal, vegetable or mineral and to go through the alphabet finding words that relate to one of those categories. Speed up the exercise so that students are compelled to think very quickly.

# RHYMES

7.3

**TIME**
20–30 minutes

**LEVEL**
Beginner/
Elementary

This is a variation of Exercise 7.2 *Words*, and involves a slightly more complex way of thinking about language. Its aim is to raise awareness of the possibilities for using rhyme in English.

## Procedure

1  Prepare the students for this exercise by discussing the way rhyme works. To get a word to rhyme with *late* for example, you need first to identify *ate* as the rhyming component and then to consider whether other possible initial letters make words that rhyme, for example:

late – ate – **pl**ate, **d**ate, **g**ate, etc.

2  The students sit in a circle. One person starts, with a word of their own choice, and the person on their right gives a word that rhymes with the first word and then adds a word of their own. The next person gives a rhyming word, and then adds their own and so on round the circle. So, for example, we might have the following pattern: *plate–mate*; *dog–log*; *sand–land*; *card–hard*, etc. When any-one cannot find a rhyme, they must make a note on paper of the word they could not find a rhyme for, give their own new word for the next person and then drop out of the circle. This continues until everyone is out or until you decide the time is up. Students who have dropped out can then ask for help to complete their missing rhyme.

# LINES

7.4

**TIME**
25–30 minutes

**LEVEL**
Beginner/
Elementary

The aim of this exercise is to provide students with the opportunity to make a text whose poetic quality results from the repetition of a simple structure.

## Procedure

1  Ask the students to concentrate on the first hour of the day. What did they do: Got up? Got washed? Got dressed? Got breakfast? Got a letter?
2  Each student should write a poem of up to ten lines, each beginning with *Got* and based on some of their daily experiences. The poems can be read aloud or displayed on the wall.

**VARIATIONS**
1  Once this routine is established, it can be repeated with other key words, such as *made*, *hope(d)*, *felt*, and can be applied to various time spans (hours, days, years) or to various situations.

**2** Another variation is to make the writing task collaborative rather than individual. Each student contributes one line which must contain a particular word – a colour word, or a key word such as *nature*, or *people*, or *angry*. Small groups can then make decisions about the best order in which to arrange the individual lines. This is a slightly more difficult writing task.

## 7.5

**TIME**
Stage 1:
30 minutes
Stage 2:
40 minutes

**LEVEL**
Beginner/
Elementary

## LIKENESS

The aim of this exercise is to raise awareness of the extent to which stylistic choice creates different effects. The exercise requires the students to use their intuitive judgment in choosing and ordering a word set according to a poetic principle which they have selected for themselves.

## Procedure

STAGE 1
1 Ask each learner to write down the sixteen longest English words they know. Explain that proper names and technical terms are also permitted.
2 Each learner turns the sixteen items into eight pairs of words. Words may be paired either for sound or sense.
3 Each learner turns the eight pairs into four two-pair 'lines', again using either the sound or sense criterion.
4 The students may read their poems aloud, but do not expect too much at this stage.

STAGE 2
5 Ask each student to select a criterion according to which they wish to choose words to make a poem. It is important that some of their sixteen words meet this criterion. You may want to suggest criteria, like only tri-syllabic words, only words beginning with a particular sound, only words that are not nouns, etc.
6 Each word that does not meet the chosen criterion should be written on a separate piece of paper (i.e. each word on its own piece) and displayed on the learner's desk. Explain that anyone who finds a word on someone else's desk that meets their criterion may take it, provided that they leave one of their unwanted words in its place. Allow ten minutes for learners to circulate swapping words in this way.
7 Allow ten more minutes for each student to arrange their words (which may be fewer than sixteen) in four 'lines'.
8 The students may read their poems aloud.

# SOUNDS THAT ARE SIMILAR

In 'The Computer's First Christmas Card', below, Edwin Morgan lists all the botched attempts a computer might make trying to say *Merry Christmas*.

**7.6**

**TIME**
30–40 minutes

**LEVEL**
Beginner/
Elementary

## THE COMPUTER'S FIRST CHRISTMAS CARD

jollymerry
hollyberry
jollyberry
merryholly
happyjolly
jollyjelly
jellybelly
bellymerry
hollyheppy
jollyMolly
marryJerry
merryHarry
hoppyBarry
heppyJarry
boppyheppy
berryjorry
jorryjelly
moppyjelly
Mollymerry
Jerryjolly
bellyboppy
jorryhoppy
hollymoppy
Barrymerry
Jarryhappy
happyboppy
boppyjolly
jollymerry
merrymerry
merrymerry
merryChris
asmerryasa
Chrismerry
asMERRYCHR
YSANTHEMUM

Edwin Morgan

Because there are no rights or wrongs in trying to generate such botched messages, the exercise that follows is modelled on Edwin Morgan's idea. Its aim is to provide the students with an opportunity to practise possible but not necessarily meaningful sound sequences in English.

## Procedure

1 Discuss the way computers sometimes print out surprising messages.

2 Read Edwin Morgan's poem and work at establishing the idea that one misprint leads naturally to the next in a sequence. Ask the class to suggest ways in which a phrase such as 'Good morning' might come out wrong. Establish the idea that tiny misprints result in phrases that are possible phonologically but are not always meaningful.

3 Ask the students to work in pairs or small groups, and distribute a well-known short phrase or the name of a well-known person to each group. The group writes a list of all the computer's botched attempts to produce it, culminating at last either in the phrase attempted or, as Edwin Morgan does, with some triumphantly wrong near miss.

## 7.7

**TIME**
30 minutes

**LEVEL**
Beginner/
Elementary

**MATERIALS**
If possible, one bottle of correction fluid per student, one copy of two short poems for each student

**SUGGESTED TEXTS**
Short, simple poems

# WORDS THAT FIT

The aim of this exercise is to draw attention to the requirements that any word in a (literary) text must meet if it is to fit into its context. It is based on allowing the learners to remove all unknown vocabulary. This technique is rarely practised by language teachers but we have found it of real benefit in lowering the affective filter and letting the learners get on with learning.

## Preparation

Choose two different short and relatively simple poems and make enough copies of each for all the students.

## Procedure

1 Pair the students and give one member of the pair one text and the other the other text. Each student whites out (or, if correction fluid is not available, blacks out) every vocabulary item whose meaning is unknown to them.

2 Ask the students to exchange texts and fill in their partner's blanked-out words with new words of their own choice.

3 Distribute the rest of the copies so that everyone has a copy of each poem. Encourage anyone with an interesting version to read it aloud.

**VARIATION**
As well as whiting out unknown items, each student writes these items down in any order on the back of the copy. Their partners can then use some or all of these words in filling in the blanks.

**SUGGESTED TEXTS**
Suitable texts for this exercise include poems as different as Roger McGough's 'Money Moans' and Walter de la Mare's 'The Listeners', as well as William Blake's 'Nurse's Song' and Julian Bell's 'Nonsense'.

## NURSE'S SONG

When the voices of children are heard on the green
And laughing is heard on the hill,
My heart is at rest within my breast
And everything else is still.

'Then come home, my children, the sun is gone down
'And the dews of night arise;
'Come, come, leave off play, and let us away
'Till the morning appears in the skies.'

'No, no, let us play, for it is yet day
'And we cannot go to sleep;
'Besides, in the sky the little birds fly
'And the hills are all cover'd with sheep.'

'Well, well, go & play till the light fades away
'And then go home to bed.'
The little ones leaped & shouted & laugh'd
And all the hills ecchoed.

William Blake

## NONSENSE

Sing a song of sixpence,
A pocketful of rye,
The lover's in the garden
The battle's in the sky.
The banker's in the city
Getting of his gold;
Oh isn't it a pity
The rye can't be sold.

The queen is drinking sherry
And dancing to a band;
A crowd may well feel merry
That it does not understand.
The banker turns his gold about
But that won't sell the rye,
Starve and grow cold without,
And ask the reason why
The guns are in the garden,
And battle's in the sky.

Julian Bell

## 7.8

**TIME**
15 minutes

**LEVEL**
Beginner/
Elementary

**MATERIALS**
Coloured card,
scissors

**CLASS SIZE**
10–20 is ideal

**SUGGESTED
TEXTS**
Short poems

# RESPONSE

This aim of this exercise, which combines reading a short poem with silent responses, is to show how a considered response to a text requires concentration. The wordless response allows time for interior monologues to take place, which may be concerned with either the meaning or the aesthetic aspects of the text.

## Preparation

Make one 'silence token' for each learner. A small round or square piece of coloured card works well. Choose a poem with approximately as many lines as there are students in the class.

## Procedure

1  Distribute one 'silence token' to each student. Explain that you are going to read the poem the class is studying out loud and that you are going to pause at the end of each line. If anyone holds their 'silence token' up at the end of a line, you will remain silent for eight seconds for each token held up. Each student may use their token only once while you are reading.
2  Allow five minutes while each student decides where they want to use their token. Their decision may be based on any criterion: the line is difficult, attractive, has associations, etc.
3  After the five-minute decision time, read the text out loud responding to the 'silence tokens'.

**NOTE**
Handled properly, silent responses contribute to the concentration and discipline of a class. They make good starter exercises with new texts, as well as good sign-off exercises after working on a text.

# PERIPHERAL LEARNING

Peripheral learning, or learning from materials present in the class-room but not directly taught to learners, is widely recognised as important (viz. maps on the walls of Geography rooms, paintings on the walls of Art rooms, etc.). Peripheral learning is also strongly stressed in Suggestopedia. Literary texts lend themselves particu-larly to peripheral learning because they are often better received when self-discovered than when directly taught.

For peripheral learning to be successful, student interaction with the peripheral materials has to take place. In the exercise that follows, we describe a Beginner-level peripheral learning experience that we have found successful, despite the apparent improbability.

## Preparation

1 Choose four or five poems which read well out loud and which are particular favourites of yours. They do not need to be especially simple or short. Each should be typed on a separate sheet.
2 For each poem, cut out at least ten pictures from colour magazines that you can associate with the text.
3 For each poem, take a large sheet of card and assemble five or six of the pictures and the text in a collage, but in such a way that there is room for further pictures to be added.
4 Cut out ten more pictures at random and put these and the pictures left over from Step 2 into a folder or cardboard box.
5 Display the collages on one wall of the classroom and place the box of pictures somewhere accessible.

## Procedure

If you are fortunate, the class will ask you what the poems are on the wall for before you have to explain. In either case, tell the class that you will read any of the texts on demand while waiting for latecomers at the beginning of a lesson. If your group is small enough, encourage them to stand with you near the text as you read. The class should also familiarise themselves with the remaining pictures and anyone who wishes may add one to any of the collages.

### VARIATIONS
There are many other ways of using literature peripherally, including ideas as simple as writing up a single line. Learner interaction with single-line texts can be promoted by encouraging the students to translate, to transliterate (i.e. translate morpheme by morpheme), to rearrange the words (see Exercise 8.4 *Variations on a text*), or to make continuations that use at least one word from the previous line.

The central point about all these peripheral approaches is that they should not be included in the part of the lesson that is formally taught, but instead should rely on learner initiative.

## 7.9

**TIME**
2 or 3 minutes at the end of break

**LEVEL**
Beginner/ Elementary

**MATERIALS**
Colour magazines, large sheets of card, glue, photo-copies of poems

**SUGGESTED TEXTS**
Your favourite poems

# CHAPTER 8

# *Advanced learners*

The exercises in this chapter are aimed at students with advanced linguistic competence. Some of them involve the creation of more complex texts, and so can be used with Chapter 6, Writing, as a second stage in the acquisition of writing skills. You can also use this chapter as a way of introducing students to advanced literary texts: Anglo-Saxon poetry, the eighteenth-century epistolary novel, science fiction, the post-modernist novel and so forth. Teachers who want to introduce students to English literature may like to use some of the exercises in this chapter with an anthology of literature or with a selection of specific books.

## 8.1

## ALPHABET POEMS

This is another exercise that utilises the alphabet and is a good way of introducing students to structural patterns based on letters of the alphabet. It takes the alphabet from Laurence Sterne's *Tristram Shandy* as an example of how a skilled writer can play with the alphabet, inventing new words and making jokes with well-known ones.

### Procedure

1 Write Sterne's text on the board:

Love is certainly, at least alphabetically speaking, one of the most
A gitating
B ewitching
C onfounded
D evilish affairs of life – the most
E xtravagant
F utilitous
G alligaskinish
H andy-dandyish
I rancundulous (there is no K to it) and
L yrical of all human passions; at the same time, the most

M isgiving
N innyhammering
O bstipating
P ragmatical
S tridulous
R idiculous – though by the bye the R should have gone first.

Allow time for a short discussion of Sterne's writing.
2 Ask the students to choose an emotion – anger, joy, grief, frustration, etc. – and following Sterne's example, to write a twenty-line
piece using twenty letters of the alphabet, one at the start of each
line. The first letter must be A. Students can shape the poem with
lines of a single word, or expand the lines if they wish following
Sterne's model. They may also experiment with words, as Sterne
does, inventing new ones if they cannot find anything suitable,
provided the structure of the poem justifies their decision.
3 Ask students to read out their poems to the group. This activity
often produces work of very high quality.

# THE GREAT LIE

**8.2**

**TIME**
20 minutes

This exercise is particularly well suited to students who are beginning
to experiment imaginatively in English. Its aim is to experiment with
creating fiction in English free from constraints of style, proper behav-
iour, politeness, etc.

**LEVEL**
Higher
intermediate +

## Procedure

**CLASS SIZE**
Preferably not
over 20

Students sit in a circle. Ask them to take ten minutes to write the
biggest lie they can think of. When the time is up each student reads
their lie aloud to the rest of the group.

**EXTENSIONS**
1 The basic exercise stands in its own right, but it can also be used as
the first stage in building more complex texts. Divide students into
pairs, and tell each pair to exchange lies, gradually making their
stories more and more extravagant and far-fetched.
2 Divide them into groups of four or five to work on linking their lies
together into some kind of fictitious whole.
3 Tell each student to pass on their lie to the next person, who then
develops it and adds another stage.

## 8.3

**TIME**
30–40 minutes

**LEVEL**
Higher
intermediate +

# ALPHABET SENTENCES

The aim of this exercise is to practise writing sequential English. It helps develop skills in synonym finding, imaginative word play and alliteration. It is a useful exercise to use as an introduction to Old English poetry where the principal device is alliteration.

## Procedure

1 Write the twenty-six letters of the English alphabet on the board. Ask students to take a large sheet of paper and write a sentence that starts with a word beginning with the letter A.
2 Tell them to pass the paper on and ask everyone to write a sentence beginning with the letter B and so on through the alphabet round the circle.
3 When the last student has written a sentence, the exercise stops regardless of the stage reached in the alphabet and everyone reads the sentences out loud to the group.

Although this can be done in the same way as the parlour game 'Consequences', i.e. after writing their sentence, each person folds the paper so that the next person does not know what has been written, it works best if students can read the preceding sentence and then write their own in the light of that reading. This often produces some interesting results: in some cases the sentences are not sequential, but in other cases the class produces a series of linked sentences that they can easily develop into a narrative.

**EXTENSION**
Ask each member of the class to choose a sentence from one of those on their papers. They then rewrite the sentence using as many words as possible that begin with the first letter. So, for example, if someone chooses a sentence that reads 'Everybody was busy in the garden planting flowers', the new sentence could be: 'Everyone excelled at excavating earth for evergreens.'

## 8.4

**TIME**
30 minutes

**LEVEL**
Higher
intermediate +

**MATERIALS**
Sheets of paper
with different
statements about
poetry on each
one

# VARIATIONS ON A TEXT

The aim of this exercise is to highlight a writer's word order options by getting the students to compose their own versions of lines of poetry using only a limited inventory of words. An example of a poem which does this is Edwin Morgan's 'Opening the Cage' which consists of fourteen lines, each a variation on the word order of 'I have nothing to say and I am saying it and that is poetry'.

## Preparation

Prepare a sheet of paper for each pair of students with either a line of poetry or a statement about poetry at the top. You need at least five or six different lines or statements so that those students who are sitting near each other will each get different ones.

## Procedure

1 Pair the students and ask them to sit in a circle. Distribute a sheet to each pair. Ask the students to reorder the words in their line or statement, write their new line below the original and pass the paper to their neighbour. Encourage them to take risks and rearrange the words creatively so as to make sentences even of doubtful grammaticality.

2 Continue until the possibilities for each line are felt to be exhausted by the students. Each text should be returned to the first pair who started the writing and can then be read aloud, discussed and displayed on the walls.

### SUGGESTED TEXTS
Suitable statements include:

- I have nothing to say and I am saying it and that is poetry.
  John Cage

- There are two kinds of writers, those who are and those who aren't.
  Karl Kraus

- We all know how difficult it is, in drawing up the simplest communication, not to say the contrary of what we mean.
  Walter Sickert

- How vain it is to sit down to write when you have not stood up to live.
  Henry David Thoreau

- In poetry everything which must be said is almost impossible to say well.
  Paul Valery

- Out of our quarrels with ourselves we make poetry.
  W B Yeats

- Science is for those who learn; poetry, for those who know.
  Joseph Roux

- Poetry is the language in which man explores his own amazement.
  Christopher Fry

- If poetry comes not as naturally as the leaves to a tree it had better not come at all.
  John Keats

  The statements above are all taken from *The Faber Book of Aphorisms*, edited by W H Auden and L Kronenberger.

### NOTE
Language is arbitrary in the sense that the words we use to convey our meanings might be, and in other languages are, different words. Similarly, the way we order them might be different: in English we say *The United States* and in French *Les Etats-Unis*. But although arbitrary,

these are the rules of a language: *dog* in English, *chien* in French; adjective before noun in English, adjective after noun in French.

These rules are of two kinds, those we must obey (it is no good saying *chien* in English and expecting people to understand) and those that allow some options and exceptions. For example, sometimes the adjective is placed after the noun in English and with interesting consequences: compare 'a responsible man' and 'the man responsible'.

Poetry often favours these options and exceptions, as anyone who has ever looked at the word order of poems will have noticed. This is one of the reasons why some linguists have categorised poetry as a deviant form of the standard language.

## 8.5

**TIME**
45–60 minutes

**LEVEL**
Advanced

# A CRISIS TWICE

This is an exercise that tests awareness of shift in register. It is a variation on a traditional ELT activity which involves teaching students how to write letters in English. The aim is to practise register shift in letter-writing. It is also a very good exercise for introducing the epistolary novel as a literary form.

## Procedure

1 Ask the students to imagine they are in a difficult situation: for example, they have just lost their job and are feeling very bad about it. They need the job and are not sure how easy it will be to get another one. Moreover, their mother is ill and must not find out about this disaster.

2 Ask the class to write a letter to a friend giving details of what has happened, being completely honest about the whole story and allowing all the feelings of anger and frustration to emerge. You can give students this task for homework if you prefer.

3 Ask the students each to write a second letter, also giving details of what has happened. This time the letter is to their mother. Tell the students that they are allowed to tell the truth in this letter, but should be careful not to hurt their mother's feelings and so may want to conceal the full impact of what has happened.

4 Ask the students to read both their letters aloud to the class and comment on the differences in style and content between the two versions.

### EXTENSION

This exercise can be taken much further. Ask students to write a third letter, for example one to a prospective employer asking for a job but stating inability to produce any references from the previous employer. Sometimes students go on to write full-length stories using the letter device.

# SUBJECTIVITY – OBJECTIVITY

The aim of this exercise is to produce two pieces of descriptive prose, one written in a supposedly 'objective' mode, the other written in a 'subjective' mode. What usually happens is that these categories dissolve during the writing. Although students may believe they are writing an 'objective piece', the others may believe they are reading a 'subjective piece'. This exposes interesting flaws in assumptions about the supposed 'objectivity' of writing and can be used to introduce more advanced narrative study.

## Procedure

1  Ask the students to write a straightforward prose description of anything they like. It is important to provide the stimulus for this. For example, send everyone to walk around in the open air for ten minutes and then write about something they have seen. The only rule is that the description must be objective. Resist the temptation to explain this term. Tell the students that they all have to work out for themselves what they understand 'objectivity' to mean. Allow them to consult a dictionary or encyclopedia if they choose.
2  When the writing has been completed, ask the students to write a second description of the same thing, but this time subjectively.
3  When both pieces are complete, split the class into groups of two or three. Taking it in turn, each member of a group shares their two pieces of writing with the others, who have to guess which is the subjective, which the objective piece. At the end of the session the groups share their findings with the whole class.

**8.6**

**TIME**
45 minutes

**LEVEL**
Advanced

# STREAMS OF CONSCIOUSNESS

Students who are used to reading conventional nineteenth-century fiction often find it very daunting when they come to tackle modernist or post-modernist writing. The aim of this exercise is to help them approach these more complex texts by enabling them to create a piece of structured stream-of-consciousness writing. An example of this kind of writing is this extract from *Ulysses* by James Joyce:

...a quarter after what an unearthly hour I suppose theyre just getting up in China now combing out their pigtails for the day well soon have the nuns ringing the angelus theyve nobody coming in to spoil their sleep except an odd priest or two for his night office the alarmclock next door at cockshout clattering the brains out of itself let me see if I can doze off 1 2 3 4 5 what kind of flowers are those...

**8.7**

**TIME**
50 minutes

**LEVEL**
Advanced

## Procedure

1 Ask the students to sit in complete silence for five minutes and use the time to try and remember a dream. Some people like to close their eyes. Complete silence and concentration are essential. Nobody should be allowed to enter the classroom during this period of intense concentration.

2 Give the students ten minutes to write down as much of the dream as they can remember. They should be urged to try and write continuously, not stopping to reflect but just writing down as much as possible on the paper before them. By the end of this stage, each student will have a fair amount of unstructured writing.

3 The next step is to transform that writing into something that someone else can read. The students work in pairs. Ask each person to exchange their dream pages with another, whose task it is to underline ten significant phrases or sentences.

4 Tell each student to take back their own piece of writing and underline their own set of ten significant phrases or sentences. These may be similar or identical to the ones chosen by the first reader, but often they are not.

5 Give each student ten minutes to write a final shortened version of the dream which must include all underlined sentences or phrases in some order and must have no punctuation.

6 Invite students to read their finished versions to the rest of the class.

**VARIATION**
Encourage students to write two versions of their dream: one in the first person, the other in the third. Some of the students will already have used one of these modes, and if they have, ask them to rewrite their piece differently.

## 8.8    BRAVE NEW WORLDS

**TIME**
60 minutes

**LEVEL**
Advanced

This is a very powerful exercise designed for use only with an advanced group that has been working together for some time. It is an exercise in communication skills, and can also serve as the starting point for advanced writing work because it stimulates thought and compels the students to confront new situations and new ideas.

It is an excellent way of introducing later discussions on difference between cultures as depicted in either satirical writing or science fiction and fantasy writing. You could ask genuinely advanced students to read Goldsmith's *A Citizen of the World* or Swift's *Gulliver's Travels*, or contemporary writers such as Ursula Le Guin, Doris Lessing, Brian Aldiss, Ray Bradbury, etc.

## Procedure

1 Explain that the group are going to create a series of new worlds. One person is to be captain of a spaceship, the others are the inhabitants of a new, undiscovered planet. Ask the person who elects to be the spaceship captain to leave the room while the rest of the group stay inside. (Each member of the group takes it in turn to go out of the room, so that everyone has a chance to experience both parts of this activity.)

Allow each group five minutes to prepare for the arrival of the alien visitor. During that time, the group have to decide on three things: (1) what their communication system is going to be (whether by signs, sounds, etc); (2) whether they are hostile or friendly to the traveller; and (3) how they can be destroyed (by touch, sound, etc. Sometimes a group who can be destroyed by touch are all killed within seconds if the spaceship captain enters the room and shakes hands, for example).

Outside the room, the space traveller has to decide whether to be hostile or friendly to the inhabitants of the planet. When the time is up, open the door and let the traveller in.

2 The encounter stage, when the traveller meets the inhabitants of the planet, usually lasts only a few minutes. The traveller has to guess what decisions the inhabitants have reached about communication, hostility and destruction. If the traveller cannot solve the problem after five minutes, then stop the activity and ask the group to explain what they have been doing.

3 Another traveller then leaves the room for five minutes, and the newly-formed group decide on another three solutions. Continue until everyone has had a turn, or until time runs out.

**EXTENSION**
Ask the class to write down their impressions of what has been going on.

# SIGNIFYING WITH SOUNDS

**8.9**

**TIME**
60 minutes

**LEVEL**
Advanced

This exercise capitalises on the way we play with sounds when we are learning a language. Frequently, adult learners are inhibited about experimenting publicly in this way. This exercise aims to show how far experimentation is possible for learners at all stages. It uses part of a text by Bob Cobbing, 'ABC in Sound', a poem which we have found to be enormously useful in the language classroom. This exercise has the double advantage of both enabling students to experiment with sound while introducing them to concrete poetry.

## Preparation

We illustrate the exercise with two sections of 'ABC in Sound': the letter
G and the letter S.

>                 grin
>                 grin
>                 grin
>                 grin
>                 grim
>         gay green
>         grey green
>         gangrene
>         ganglia
>                 grin
>                 grin
>                 grin

S i g n
S o u n d
S e n s e
S y m b o l
S i g n a l
S p e e c h
S y m p t o m
S y l l a b l e
S e m i o s i s
S t r u c t u r e
S e m a n t i c s
S e m i o t i c s
S i g n s t o c k
S y n c h r o n i c
S y n t a c t i c s
S i g n s y s t e m
S i g n a g g r e g a t e
S i g n i n v e n t o r y
S y l l a b o g r a p h y
S i g n c o l l e c t i v e
S y n o n y m i c s i g n s
S y m b o l i c i n d i c a t o r
S y m b o l i c u s u r p a t i o n
S e m a n t i c d i f f e r e n t i a l
S u p p o r t i n g r e d u n d a n c y
S o c i a l l y i n s t i t u t i o n a l i z e d
S y s t e m a t i c w h o l e o f s p e e c h s o u n d s

S h i t

Bob Cobbing

## Procedure

1 Read the poems, then ask the students to select a letter of the alphabet at random and to spend just three minutes writing every noun and verb they can think of that begins with that letter.
2 Ask them to write every place name that begins with that letter for a further three minutes.
3 Ask them to write every proper name that begins with the letter for a further three minutes.
4 Ask them to write every adjective and adverb that begins with the letter for a further three minutes.
5 Ask them to write anything else they can think of that begins with the letter for the final three minutes. The students have now been writing lists of words for fifteen minutes non-stop.
6 Ask the students to write a short sentence composed of words starting with their chosen letter that will act as a memory aid in teaching the alphabet (e.g. 'A is for appetising apples . . .', 'J is for jubilation among judicious judges . . .', etc.) and which utilises some of the words in their list.
7 After this simple exercise in structuring, ask students to select some more of the words (it is best not to impose any restrictions on the number here) and write a ten- or fifteen-line piece following the examples of the two poems provided. This stage can produce some surprisingly good results. Some people prefer to keep their texts short and succinct, others prefer to make them longer.

# EVERYDAY RHYTHMS

This exercise helps students to become more aware of the prosody or rhythm of verse by using it to express everyday ideas. It draws attention to the fact that in verse stresses additional to those found in standard language may occur.

## Preparation

Take (a verse of) the poem you are reading in class and copy each line on to a separate piece of paper. On the reverse of each sheet write a single line parody in everyday language that has exactly the same prosody. Mark in the stresses. The ideas expressed in the parody should be as mundane as possible. The following examples (with stresses shown in bold) show how the activity might work.

**8.10**

TIME
30–40 minutes

LEVEL
Higher
intermediate +

SUGGESTED
TEXTS
Any poem with a
regular meter

- *Iambic pentameter:*
  But **thy** et**er**nal **sum**mer **shall** not **fade** (Shakespeare)
  So **Jane's** ap**point**ment **is** at **four** o'**clock** (parody)
- *Ballad metre:*
  When **Rob**in **Hood** and **Lit**tle **John**
  Went **o'er** yon **bank** of **broom** (original)
  What**ev**er **Ja**net's **sis**ter **says**
  Will **al**ways **be** spot **on** (parody)
- *Four iambic feet:*
  For **oft** when **on** my **couch** I **lie** (Wordsworth, 'Daffodils')
  Has **any**one had **break**fast **yet** (parody)

## Procedure

1 Group or pair the students and give each group one of the prepared sheets, parody side up. Each group then produces their own line or sentence but with exactly the same prosodic structure as the parody. They should not look at the original line on the other side of the paper.

2 The sheets are passed from group to group with each group adding a further line.

3 When four or five lines have been written, ask the groups to turn the papers over. Allow five minutes for them to practise reading the original and the parodies out loud, assigning the same pitch prominences and quantities to each. Ask a reader from each group to read their lines aloud to the class. You will have to provide some guidance at this stage.

### NOTE

Even some native speakers have problems hearing prosody. For the non-native speaker, these problems are greatly magnified. This is especially true in a generally stress-timed language like English where the pitch prominences and the quantities or vowel lengths we assign are often context determined and not therefore learnable in advance. As an illustration, notice how the two *how cans* are differently stressed in W B Yeats's poem 'Leda and the Swan':

How can (haʊ ˈkæn) those terrified vague fingers push
The feathered glory from her loosening thighs?
And how can (ˈhaʊ kən) body laid in that white rush,
But feel the strange heart beating where it lies?

# PROVERBS OF HELL

**8.11**

**TIME**
35 minutes

**LEVEL**
Higher
intermediate +

**MATERIALS**
A small unruled
card or similarly
sized piece of
paper for each
student

The aim of this exercise is to try to understand texts that have a paradoxical, riddle-like quality. One of the strengths of the exercise is that the two proverbs that each student works with are likely to make a lasting impact and be committed to memory.

## Preparation

Prepare one card, index card or small piece of paper for each student by copying on to it one of Blake's 'Proverbs of Hell' (see below). Copy a different proverb on to each card.

PROVERBS OF HELL

In seed time learn, in harvest teach, in winter enjoy.
Drive your cart and your plough over the bones of the dead.
The road of excess leads to the palace of wisdom.
The cut worm forgives the plough.
Dip him in the river who loves water.
A fool sees not the same tree that a wise man sees.
He whose face gives no light, shall never become a star.
Eternity is in love with the productions of time.
The busy bee has no time for sorrow.
The hours of folly are measured by the clock; but of wisdom, no
clock can measure.
All wholesome food is caught without a net or a trap.
No bird soars too high, if he soars with his own wings.
A dead body revenges not injuries.
If the fool would persist in his folly he would become wise.
Prisons are built with stones of Law, brothels with bricks of Religion.
The pride of the peacock is the glory of God.
The lust of the goat is the bounty of God.
The wrath of the lion is the wisdom of God.
The nakedness of woman is the work of God.
The bird a nest, the spider a web, man friendship.
What is now proved was once only imagined.
The cistern contains: the fountain overflows.
Always be ready to speak your mind, and a base man will avoid you.
Everything possible to be believed is an image of truth.
The eagle never lost so much time as when he submitted to learn of the crow.
He who has suffered you to impose on him, knows you.
The tigers of wrath are wiser than the horses of instruction.
Expect poison from the standing water.
You never know what is enough unless you know what is more than enough.
The apple tree never asks the beech how he shall grow; nor the lion
the horse how he shall take his prey.
If others had not been foolish, we should be so.
The best wine is the oldest, the best water the newest.

The crow wished everything was black, the owl that everything was white.
If the lion was advised by the fox, he would be cunning.
Sooner murder an infant in its cradle than nurse unacted desires.
Truth can never be told so as to be understood and not be believed.

William Blake

## Procedure

1 Arrange the students in a circle. Distribute one card to each student and ask them to write their own version of the proverb on the other side of it. Blake's original idea should be retained, but the students' versions may be close or very different. For example, 'The cut worm forgives the plough' → 'The smashed caterpillar forgives the combine harvester' (close), or 'Do not expect a broken bottle to take revenge' (different).

2 Collect the cards and redistribute them round the circle so that everyone has someone else's. Allow students two or three minutes to prepare to read the proverbs out loud in a fluent manner.

3 Tell the students that you will read the two proverbs on your card. You will not say whether you are reading Blake's or your own version first. Any student with proverbs that are related to yours in theme or content should read next. This process should continue without you intervening again until everyone has read their proverbs out loud.

### VARIATIONS

1 For a variation at elementary and intermediate level, see Exercise 5.4 *Wise sayings*.

2 Instead of reading the proverbs round the class, play dominoes with them. To do this, at the Preparation stage, divide one side of the card down the middle and write Blake's proverb on the left-hand side. At Step 1, instruct the students to write their version on the right-hand half:

| Blake's proverb | Student's version |
|---|---|

Collect in and distribute the cards as in Step 2. Start playing dominoes (Step 3) by laying your card down. Anyone who wants to place their card next to yours must explain why they relate to each other. This process is repeated until as many of the cards as possible are placed in the sequence. This takes considerably longer than reading the cards out loud round the class – allow twenty minutes extra.

ACKNOWLEDGEMENT
The domino idea (Variation 2) is David Hill's.

# WRITING THE UNWRITABLE

This exercise tackles a very problematic aspect of literary study: the reading of texts that are on the boundaries of good taste and social acceptability. The example text is a well-known war poem which shocks through its brevity and simplicity.

**IT IS NOT DEATH**

It is not death
  Without hereafter
To one in dearth
  Of life and its laughter,

Nor the sweet murder
  Dealt slow and even
Unto the martyr
  Smiling at heaven:

It is the smile
  Faint as a [waning] myth,
Faint, and exceeding small
  On a boy's murdered mouth.

Wilfred Owen

## 8.12

**TIME**
45–60 minutes

**LEVEL**
Advanced

## Procedure

1 Read the poem to the students, and lead a short discussion. This usually raises questions about the role of poetry in a society, and whether poetry should principally concern itself with the beautiful rather than the horrible.
2 Divide the students into pairs and ask each person to take it in turn to tell the other person about something they feel is unpleasant but too important to be ignored. Each one of the pair tells a story to the other for no more than five minutes, and the listener must make notes. Frequently the stories involve newspaper items, but sometimes personal experiences.
3 Ask students to write a five-line piece (either a poem or a string of five sentences) based on their notes or their partner's story. The person who told the story must *not* write about their own story; they must write about the story they have heard. This is important, because the exercise is about the structuring of intense experience into language, and is not meant to be personal therapy. If students write about their own story there is a danger that the emotions will take over and the exercise will be of little use as a language learning experience.
4 Finally, ask each person to read their piece aloud to the class.

## 8.13

**TIME**
30 minutes
reading time + 30
minutes for
discussion

**LEVEL**
Higher
intermediate +

**MATERIALS**
Copies of a
specially prepared
text

**SUGGESTED
TEXTS**
Stories, and
poems that tell
stories

# DISCUSSING A TEXT

Most teachers agree that if discussions are to work in the language classroom, they should to some extent be structured. In other words, it is not safe to assume that a discussion will be self-sustaining, although it is obviously good to encourage this sort of free-flowing talk when possible. Structuring discussions involves giving everyone a role, drawing on the students' own experience and knowledge and breaking larger classes into smaller groups in which more equal contributions are possible.

No discussion of a literary text will work unless the text itself has been carefully read and is already well understood. This exercise is divided into two parts: a reading task followed by a set of structured discussion topics. One purpose of the discussion is to deepen the existing understanding of the poem. The overall aim is to use a literary text as the basis of a carefully structured discussion of a non-literary kind.

## Preparation

We illustrate below the quality and quantity of preparation needed for a structured discussion based on a literary text in the way we work with Philip Larkin's poem 'Wild Oats'. This involves preparing the text for the reading task and thinking out a set of questions to facilitate the discussion. A similar degree of preparation will be needed for any text you choose to work with. The words in brackets are the words omitted which the students try to supply.

WILD OATS

| | |
|---|---|
| About twenty years ago | |
| Two girls came in where I worked — | |
| A.............English Rose | [bosomy] |
| And............................I could talk to. | [her friend in specs] |
| Faces in those days sparked | |
| The whole shooting match off, and I doubt | |
| If ever one had like hers: | |
| But it was the friend I took out. | |
| | |
| And in seven years after that | |
| Wrote over four hundred letters | |
| Gave a...................... | [ten guinea ring] |
| I got back in the end, and met | |
| At numerous cathedral cities | |
| Unknown to the clergy. I believe | |
| I met beautiful twice. She was trying | |
| Both times (so I thought) not to........ | [laugh] |

Parting, after about five
Rehearsals, was an agreement
That I was too........, withdrawn                    [selfish]
And easily..........to love.                          [bored]
Well, useful to get that learnt.
In my wallet there are still two snaps
Of......................with fur gloves on.          [Bosomy Rose]
Unlucky charm,.............                            [perhaps]

Philip Larkin

## Procedure

STAGE 1: READING

1 Distribute copies of the prepared text. Ask the students to work first
  individually (for ten minutes) and then in small groups (for ten
  minutes), trying to decide how to fill in the gaps.
2 Allow a further ten minutes for going over the text listening to
  suggestions, supplying the original words and making sure that the
  students understand the relationships between the three people in
  the poem.

STAGE 2: DISCUSSION

First, it is a good thing to establish names for the three characters. For
example, 'Bosomy Rose', 'The Friend in Specs' and 'The Bloke' or, if
you prefer, 'Him'.

Your role in facilitating the structured discussion is to set up
situations and to ask the kind of questions that ensure the students do
the talking. Here are some suggestions for this text:

1 'If you had to be one of the three people in the poem, which would
  you choose to be?' Make the students think carefully about their
  choice and write it down in silence. This ensures that each student
  decides for themselves. One possible follow-up would be to make up
  little groups of different characters and try to get them to convert
  each other.
2 You might decide to divide a large class into small groups (for
  example, according to who the students sympathise with; Bosomy
  Rose, The Friend in Specs, The Bloke). Small groups often make it
  possible for everyone to play a part in the discussion.
3 'Is there anything in your chosen character's personality or behav-
  iour that disturbs you?' You could put (one of) the characters 'on
  trial' with the class or group acting as a jury to acquit or convict.
4 Particular questions about each character:
  i Is she right to ditch him?
  ii What do you think about his attitude to the experience?
  iii Why does 'beautiful' go around with a plain friend?
  These questions can be approached more formally, with groups
  preparing attacking and defensive statements.

5 'Which of the characters do you (a) like, and (b) dislike the most?'
6 'Have you ever had an experience similar to those of any of the characters in the poem?'
7 'Do you agree that he compromises himself by going out with the plain girl?' Further questions leading out of this might include: 'Have you ever done such a thing?' 'Is it a right or a wrong thing to do?' 'Ought one only to have such a relationship with someone for whom one has genuinely deep feelings?'
8 'Or is he being realistic? Is there a biological principle that brings a beautiful person together with another beautiful person and a less beautiful with another less beautiful? Are the married people you know or the famous married people one reads about in newspapers and magazines usually similar to each other or not?'
9 'Is it better to marry someone similar to or different from you?'
Although you may not work through all your prepared questions, it is often best to limit a discussion to thirty minutes.

OPTIONAL STAGE 3: WRITING
1 All this happened between thirteen and twenty years ago. How might either of the two women look back on the incident now?
2 Write a poem, or a diary or a series of letters telling the story from the fiancée's point of view.
3 Reflect on a past experience and call the poem or story 'Perhaps'.
4 Compare this relationship with a romantic relationship such as the wedding of two film-stars or a marriage in a Shakespearean comedy. Which is closest to real life and why? Are people more likely to be happy in a romantic or a realistic relationship?

# Bibliography

Ely, P 1984 *Bring the Language Lab back to Life* Pergamon
Gattegno, C 1972 *Teaching Foreign Languages in Schools: The Silent Way* Educational Solutions
Gattegno, C 1976 *The Common Sense of Teaching Foreign Languages* Educational Solutions
Morgan, J and Rinvolucri, M 1986 *Vocabulary* OUP
Ngugi wa Thiong'o 1986 'Literature in schools' in Brumfit, C J and Carter, R A (Eds) *Literature and Language Teaching* OUP
Nunan, D 1988a *The Learner-centered Curriculum* CUP
Nunan, D 1988b *Syllabus Design* OUP
Palmer, B 1984 *The Literary Practice Book* University of East Anglia
Pechou, A 1985 *The Poet and the Scientists* Pilgrims Publications
Pratt, M L 1987 'Linguistic Utopias' in Fabb, N, Attridge, D, Durant, A and MacCabe, C (Eds) *The Linguistics of Writing* University of Manchester Press
Thomas, J A 1983 'Cross-cultural pragmatic failure'. *Applied Linguistics* 4(2): 91–112